Better Vocabulary in 30 Minutes a Day

By
Edie Schwager

CAREER PRESS
3 Tice Road
P.O. Box 687
Franklin Lakes, NJ 07417
1-800-CAREER-1
201-848-0310 (NJ and outside U.S.)
FAX: 201-848-1727

BETTER VOCABULARY IN 30 MINUTES A DAY

ISBN 1-56414-247-7, $8.99

Cover design by L & B Desktop Publishing & Printing

Printed in the U.S.A. by Book-mart Press

To order this title by mail, please include price as noted above, $2.50 handling per order, and $1.00 for each book ordered. Send to: Career Press, Inc., 3 Tice Road, P.O. Box 687, Franklin Lakes, NJ 07417.

Or call toll-free 1-800-CAREER-1 (NJ and Canada: 201-848-0310) to order using VISA or MasterCard, or for further information on books from Career Press.

Library of Congress Cataloging-in-Publication Data

Schwager, Edith.
    Better vocabulary in 30 minutes a day / by Edie Schwager.
       p.   cm. -- (Better English series)
    ISBN 1-56414-247-7 (pbk.)
    1. Vocabulary.   I. Title.   II. Series.
PE1449.S4545   1996
    428.1--dc20

                                                            96-21262
                                                                CIP

Acknowledgments

My heartfelt thanks go to Michael J. Schwager, who happens to be my son and is also a fellow writer and editor. Besides his pursuits as an author and writing consultant, he's a computer guru. He offered insightful suggestions about the text and helped make sure that the book got to Career Press on time, and in the electronic form the publisher needed.

Special thanks go to Doris S. Michaels, my literary agent, for her diligence, competence, patience and generosity of spirit. I received the assignment to write this book because of her, and her enthusiasm motivated me from our first conversation about the project to the last word.

My father, Michael Cohen, always told me that if you're going to do a job, do it right, no matter what it is. Above everything except family, he revered education and learning. He taught me by example that one of the highest human endeavors is gathering knowledge and using it to exercise wisdom. This book is dedicated to his memory.

So hats off to all the Michaels!

Thanks to everyone at Career Press—especially Ron Fry, president; Betsy Sheldon, editor in chief; Ellen Scher, associate editor; Jane A. Brody, editor; and Fred Nachbaur, marketing manager—for their encouragement and all their efforts.

Contents

Preface 7

Key To Abbreviations 17

Words Are Tools 19

Word Roots 157

Word Acrobics 181

Preface

Eating potato chips

Have you ever noticed that you can't look up just one word? It's like eating potato chips. You can never eat just one. Before you catch yourself, your eye spies another word whose meaning you want to know, and that entices you to look up that one, too. This never-ending process is called enriching your mind.

This book will help you by adding to your vocabulary. It will encourage you to use words correctly and confidently, as dynamic tools that explain or persuade.

Whether English is your native language or your second language, your constant use of this book will accomplish several things: It will stimulate you to become interested in the meanings and origins of words, introduce you to new ideas and concepts, acquaint you with the fun and mystery of mythology and history, and add to the sum of your knowledge.

The Athenian playwright Aristophanes (c. 450-385 BC) wrote that "by words, the mind is excited and the spirit elated."

Much more recently, H. G. Wells, author of *The Time Machine* and other futuristic novels, wrote that "human history becomes more and more a race between education and catastrophe" (*The Outline of History*, 1920).

The ultimate tools

Words can work magic. Despite generals, wars are not won on the battlefield. Eventually, all sides have to sit down at the negotiating table. Wars are finally won with words.

Most human transactions are won or lost through words.

Only humans have a written language

Only human beings have the ability to use a system of words to convey ideas—that is, to communicate with language. Other animals can communicate to one another (for instance, with certain sounds or body movements), but not with words. Only we humans have that power.

Expressing yourself well

The way you express yourself is your showcase to the world. To use another figure of speech, it's the window through which your family, your friends, your teacher, your colleagues and the rest of the world perceive you.

It's within your power to create the image you want to present. Your words are as important as your actions, and are often more memorable.

People who are good conversationalists, who can express themselves grammatically and understandably, are in a more favorable life situation.

People who can write clearly, without ambiguity, are pearls of great price.

Opening your mind to new challenges, new ideas and new words can be one of the most exciting and pleasurable intellectual experiences you'll ever have. One effective way to do that is by using this book diligently.

What is English?

Our language didn't come out of thin air. It's an amalgam, a glorious intermingling of words that originated with diverse cultures, tastes, styles and manners.

Most of our simpler and more practical words come from the Germanic and Scandinavian side of our language heritage. It will not escape your notice that the majority of the etymologies in this book's entries contain the abbreviations *L* (Latin) and *Gk* (Greek). That's because most words having to do with culture and learning come from Latin and Greek roots. In addition, almost the entire English medical and scientific vocabulary comes from Latin and Greek.

English has thousands of borrowings from other languages as well. Those are among the most exotic words— for example, *harem, mikado, bazaar, kiosk*. French has contributed more than 15,000 words to English. Spanish and Italian were also generous. The Netherlands gave us words having to do with the shipbuilding and shipping industries. Scandinavian warriors invading and then settling in the Danelaw area of England brought words that became part of the language.

After the conquest of England by the Normans in 1066, French became the country's official language, but the common people continued to speak English. Between 1066 and the 14th century, a dialect of French intermixed with English known as Anglo-French became the official language, and the language of the court and the law. Over the centuries, these words were intermixed with the Germanic and other words that already existed in English.

How did English evolve into the language as we know it? That's a subject that would fill an entire library, but it helps to know that English owes a great deal to Romance languages such as Portuguese, Italian, French, Spanish and Romanian. The Netherlands, the Scandinavian and Slavic countries, and other European cultures also contributed substantially to our vocabulary.

Robert Burchfield, in *The English Language*, wrote that "every major historical, political, and social event, every discovery and every new belief, since *c.* 450 has brought change to the English language, and not least to the meanings of words."

Evolution and revolution

Language changes, the meanings of words change, politics, styles and cultures change. We all benefit by and contribute to these developments.

More scientific, medical and technologic advances have taken place in the past 100 years than in all the preceding centuries put together. Fortunately, our language is flexible and capacious enough to absorb these changes and to build new terms on them.

In every country the common people—workers, artisans, business people—make the everyday practical language, the vulgate. Others, such as the engineers, artists, physicians, and scientists, contribute the more technical and specific terms. Thus the language grows and changes.

Idiosyncratic idioms

English is an extremely idiomatic language, full of colorful and vivid imagery. We use phrases without a second thought as to their literal meaning. Language evolves through interactions between and among humans. Although we think in words, our actions take place without conscious thought as to how they are to be expressed in spoken language.

When we say something is "as easy as pie," we're not thinking about pie at all. "Holding your own" *what*? People in my area go on vacation not "down to" the shore but "down the shore," even though the Atlantic Ocean is more east of here than south.

So the idioms go. They don't have to be logical. That's just the way it is. However, language in general has to be logical if it is to be communicated effectively.

Some idioms, like humans, have a life. They are born, they flourish, and then they die. Others remain with us for centuries, usually because there is a contemporaneous use for them.

Although we use idiom constantly in both written and spoken language, writing gives us the golden opportunity to use logic too. Good writing presupposes clear thinking. Knowing the right words gives us, as the idiom goes, a leg up.

I never make misteaks

Words have shades and hues of meaning, subtleties and nuances. Many errors are caused by the irrational, irritating, unphonetic and difficult spelling of English words. These characteristics make learning English tough, especially for nonnative speakers. The difficulty is compounded by the innumerable *homonyms* and *homophones* in English, words that sound or look alike but mean different things. The section called "Word Roots" contains several examples.

Other difficulties arise when people who were reared where British English reigns supreme immigrate to this country and have to contend with American English spelling. Still other mistakes stem from poor reading (or *no* reading) or studying habits, substandard education, lack of access to a library, lack of a personal library and, above all, a lack of interest or motivation, otherwise known as *apathy*.

English is the world's lingua franca

There is no world language, and there may never be, but English approaches it. It is the language used to record more than 80 percent of the world's computer information.

English is the lingua franca, the commercial language, of the world. If you want to do business abroad, you must know English. If you want to venture into the international computer networks, you must know English.

Here's your user's manual!

In the main section of this book, "Words Are Tools," the lexicon is arranged alphabetically, so that you'll be able to find the exact word you want quickly and easily, without being distracted or interrupted by other sections.

The illustrative sentences give you a good idea of how each word can be used in context. For instance, when the entry is a verb, the corresponding noun or adjective is also given.

The section titled "Word Roots," also arranged alphabetically, will help you build your vocabulary using an architectural style. You'll soon be able to figure out the meanings of unfamiliar words by recognizing the roots and their affixes. You already know many of them, so you can concentrate on the words you don't see every day. Prefixes and suffixes are collectively known in the trade as *affixes*.

Some definitions in "Words Are Tools" are informal, to get a point or two across. Ditto for "Word Roots" and my commentaries.

You will note that some words in one section are repeated in another. That's for memory reinforcement and refreshment.

Diacritical or accent marks are not used in words that have already been integrated into the English language.

Note the "Key to Abbreviations" used in the book: F, Gk, Ger, F, L, ME, ISV, etc. You'll find it just before the main section of this book.

And, finally, at the end of the book, a chance to practice your new vocabulary skills! You can undoubtedly figure out what "Word Aerobics" are. I coined this phrase because that kind of exercise is challenging and a lot of fun for me.

Look it up!

Mark Twain, who was noted for his zingers, wrote, "The man who does not read good books has no advantage over the man who cannot read them." That goes for women too.

Guessing at what a word means works sometimes, but beware of fake (fake folk) etymology. In the words profession, this alert is called a caveat, as in caveat emptor, which means "Buyer, beware!" For instance, words that contain ped can refer to feet (pedal, biped, pedicure), children (pediatrics), teaching (pedagogy, pedantry), or lousiness (pediculosis). Not to mention soils (pedogeography) or botany (peduncle, which has nothing to do with relatives but is a flower-bearing stalk).

English is an extremely versatile language. One word can have many meanings: Consider the word *down*. You think it's a simple word, but if you look it up in the *big* dictionary, *Webster's Third New International Dictionary of the English Language*, you'll see that the entries for this little word consume an inordinate amount of space. It can be several parts of speech: a noun (*down* off a duck, ups and *downs*, the *downs* of England's countryside); an adjective (the computers are *down* again, *down* payment); an adverb (tore the Sears building *down*, keeping your expenses *down*, kept *down* by lack of education); a preposition (perspiration dripping *down* his T-shirt, went *down* the mountain); or a verb (*downed* by a superior wrestler, *down* the soda pop too quickly, *down* the tools in a sitdown strike).

Innumerable other words in our language can be several different parts of speech.

The watchphrase is **look it up!**

The best and the brightest

In my work I depend on the monumentally scholarly Merriam-Webster books, notably the following:

- *Webster's Third New International Dictionary of the English Language, Unabridged*, known briefly and affectionately in this book as *Webster's Third*.

- *Webster's New Biographical Dictionary*.

- *Webster's Word Histories*.

In addition, I find *Bartlett's Familar Quotations*, 16th ed., edited by Justin Kaplan, and several other excellent books of quotations indispensable resources.

The other books in my voluminous (no pun intended) library that I used in writing this book are too numerous to mention. Some day I hope to catalog them. (I should live so long.)

I am eternally grateful to these wonderful scholars and all the other lexicographers, philologists, etymologists, linguists and verbophiles who have contributed immeasurably to our vibrant, vigorous and *living* language.

The next move

The ball's in your court. As you use this book, you'll find that you can comprehend and will be familiar with terms used in, for example, *The New York Times*, which is one of the best newspapers in the world and certainly one of the best edited. Many words in this book are straight out of *The Times*, since it has always been the Gold Standard for me. Naturally, any single work such as this book can only scratch the surface. It's up to you to prospect deeper for more gold.

As you increase and improve your vocabulary, you'll also find that you're more confident and comfortable in your speech. Your reading and writing will come much easier. Success in your life may very well hinge on your ability to communicate lucidly and powerfully. I don't necessarily mean monetary success; social and artistic success is every bit as important for fulfillment.

Alexander Pope wrote:

A little learning is a dangerous thing;
Drink deep, or taste not the Pierian spring:
There shallow draughts intoxicate the brain,
And drinking largely sobers us again.

Pope also wrote:

True ease in writing comes from art, not chance,
As those move easiest who have learn'd to dance.
'Tis not enough no harshness gives offence,
The sound must seem an echo to the sense.

You, too, can learn to dance.
Never stop learning.

Key To Abbreviations

AF	Anglo-French
Ar	Arabic
E	English
F	French
Ger	German
Gk	Greek
Heb	Hebrew
ISV	International Scientific Vocabulary
It	Italian
L	Latin
LHeb	Late Hebrew
LL	Late Latin
ME	Middle English
MF	Middle French
ML	Medieval Latin
NL	New Latin
OE	Old English
OF	Old French
OHG	Old High German
OL	Old Latin
ONF	Old North French
OSp	Old Spanish
Russ	Russian
Skt	Sanskrit
Sp	Spanish
Sw	Swedish
Y	Yiddish

A

abridge—to shorten, abbreviate (from L *ad*, toward, *breviare*, to abbreviate)

> *It's easy to write a long memo. To **abridge** it usually takes much longer.*
>
> *The collegiate dictionaries are **abridgments** of larger works.*

In American English, *fledgling*, *acknowledgment* and *judgment*, like **abridgment**, are spelled without an *e* after the *g*, although *abridgement* is also correct. The British style generally is to retain the *e* in these and similar words.

Synonyms for **abridgment** include *abstract*, *brief* and *epitome*.

Blaise Pascal summed it up when he wrote (in 1657), "I have made this letter longer than usual because I lack the time to make it shorter."

abrogate—to give up, repeal, set aside (L *ab*, from, *rogare*, to ask)

> *Constantine refused when asked to **abrogate** his throne.*
>
> *Free citizens should not **abrogate** their rights under the Constitution.*

*Treaties are sometimes **abrogated** by irresponsible nations.*

Synonyms for **abrogate** include *annul, void* and *nullify.*

abstinence—self-denial, abstaining (OF, from L *abstinentia*)

*Some religions prescribe **abstinence** from alcohol and certain foods during holy days.*
***Abstinence** does not always make the heart grow fonder.*

The verb is **to abstain**.

abstruse—hard to understand, concealed, mysterious (from L *abstrusus*, hidden)

*The workings of statisticians are too **abstruse** for those of us who are unfamiliar with mathematics.*
*Many worthwhile subjects are **abstruse** until you start to study them.*

accretion—increase, increment, accumulation (from L *accretio*, increase)

*The United States was formed by **accretion** of land bought or otherwise acquired from other countries.*
*The **accretion** of sand dunes takes eons, but can be undone by one hurricane.*

Carl Sandburg wrote that "the United States *is*, not *are*. The Civil War was fought over a verb."

acerbic—(a-SIR-bik) acid, biting, sarcastic (from L *acerbus, acer,* sharp)

> *Groucho Marx was celebrated for his* **acerbic** *wit as well as his rolling eyes, fake mustache and meaningful leer. In one of his motion pictures, he said, "I never forget a face, but in your case I'll make an exception."*
>
> *The district attorney was notorious for his* **acerbic** *dueling with defense lawyers.*
>
> *The film* Laura *featured Clifton Webb as the* **acerbic** *Waldo Lydecker, a critic in the full sense of the word.*

acme—peak, the top, the best (Gk *akme,* highest point)

> *Known as the "Waltz King" and the composer of the immortal "The Beautiful Blue Danube," Johann Strauss was considered the* **acme** *of waltz composers.*
>
> *Levi Strauss invented the* **acme** *of jeans.*
>
> *Vintage grapes reach their* **acme** *when climatic conditions are also at their* **acme***.*

Wiley Coyote, the Roadrunner's nemesis in Loony Tunes cartoons, favored products made by the **Acme** company, but they never performed to his satisfaction.

acrimony—bitterness, rancor, sharpness (MF *acrimonie,* from L *acer,* sharp, *acrimonia*)

> *Debates in the Congress are often full of* **acrimony** *rather than reason.*
>
> *Alimony payments are sometimes accompanied by* **acrimony***.*

acrophobia—fear of heights (Gk *akros*, topmost, extreme, L and Gk *phobia*, abnormal fear)

> *She has never visited the Grand Canyon or Sandia Mountain because she has **acrophobia**.*

> Some people refuse to fly in airplanes. They're not afraid to fly—they're just afraid of heights.

acropolis—city on a height (Gk *acr*, topmost, *polis*, city)

> *The magnificent Parthenon in Athens is the main attraction on the **Acropolis**.*
> *There are many other temples on the **Acropolis**, but the Parthenon is the most world-renowned. It has undergone considerable renovation to restore the damage caused by acid rain, earthquakes and millions of visitors.*

adamant—unyielding, inflexible, stubborn (L *adamas*, steel, hardest gem, diamond)

> *We are persistent in our beliefs; others are **adamant**.*
> *To be **adamant** in the face of logic is fruitless.*

> **Adamantine** is a synonym for **adamant**.

adherent—follower, advocate, proponent (MF *adhérent*, from L *adhaerens*)

> *He was a firm **adherent** of the Teddy Roosevelt philosophy of government: "Speak softly and carry a big stick; you will go far."*

> This word is also an adjective:

*An ingenious invention, Velcro, is an **adherent** hook-and-loop tape.*

Returning from a walk in the Swiss countryside in the early 1950s, George deMescal found cockleburs on his jacket. He wondered what made them so tenacious. When he examined the prickly plants under the microscope, he saw that cockleburs are covered with hooks, and that they became embedded in his jacket.

Velcro is used in aerospace and other applications.

The name Velcro comes from *vel*vet and *cro*chet.

adverse—unfavorable, unfortunate, critical (MF, from L *adversus*)

*Under **adverse** weather conditions, Jason sailed off in the Argos with his brave companions for the adventure of his life.*

*The playwright was visibly downcast when he read the **adverse** reviews of his latest work.*

Don't confuse this with *averse*, which means having a feeling of distaste, repugnance, dislike or antipathy.

aegis—(EE-jis) protection, auspices, leadership (L, from Gk *aigis*, shield of Zeus)

*The task force operated under the **aegis** of the United Nations.*

*Under the **aegis** of the Czarina, Rasputin became the power behind the throne.*

Zeus, the top brass in Greek mythology, wore an **aegis**, a shield or breastplate. His daughter, also wore a symbol of their preeminence. The shields were made of *aigis*, which originally meant goatskin. The symbolic meaning has been extended to auspices or sponsorship.

aggregation—a grouping together (L *ad*, to, *grex*, herd, flock)

*New Jersey probably has the largest **aggregation** of pharmaceutical firms in the United States.*

*Arthur Goldberg became general counsel for the **aggregation** of local unions known as the Congress of Industrial Organizations.*

agoraphobia—fear of crowds or open spaces (Gk *agora*, assembly, marketplace, *phobia*, abnormal fear)

*The recluse was afflicted with **agoraphobia**, which prevented him from leaving his home for years at a time.*

People with **agoraphobia** are afraid of being embarrassed or caught helpless in crowds or in the midst of an open space.

This word came into general use in 1873 with publication of an article by Dr. C. Westphal, and became part of the psychological and psychiatric lexicons.

alar—wing, winglike (L *ala*, wing)

*Angels are usually portrayed with spectacular **alar** appendages.*

This is a handy four-letter word for crossword puzzle and Scrabble fans. The plural of *ala* (wing) is *alae*. A synonym for winged or **alar** is *alate*.

aleatoric—improvisatory, random, chancy (L alea, die, dice)

*Life is full of **aleatoric** events.*

Composer John Cage is preeminent in the field of **aleatoric** *music.*

A favorite pastime of the ancient Romans was gambling with dice. Julius Caesar, on crossing the Rubicon, said, *"Iacta alea est!"* "The die is cast!" His gamble eventually paid off with a tremendous military victory.

alternative—a choice or option (L *alternus*, interchangeable)

> *Lord Cardigan's order apparently gave the Light Brigade no* **alternative** *to charging the Russian lines at Balaclava.*
>
> *Desmond had three* **alternatives**: *He could go to college, enter the NBA draft system or choose a business career.*

This word should be distinguished from *alternate*, which means by turns, or one after the other. Traffic reports give "alternate" routes when they should be giving **alternative** routes.

The plural **alternatives** reminds me of the story about the devoted son who came to his mother's home to thank her for the two neckties she had given him for his birthday. When he entered the house, he saw her face fall. "Hi, mom. Something wrong?" he asked. She answered with another question: "What's the matter? You didn't like the *other* tie?"

ambidextrous—skillful with either hand (L *ambi*, both, *dexter*, on the right, skillful)

> *Plumbers and other artisans are* **ambidextrous** *because they have to be able to work in any uncomfortable position with either hand.*

*Foreign correspondents must be not only inquisitive—they must be politically **ambidextrous** as well.*

Although left-handed people were as skillful or talented as the right-handed in ancient Rome (as they still are), the bias in Latin is plain to see. This word is often used metaphorically to mean versatile or flexible.

ambience—surrounding atmosphere, environment, etc. (F *ambiant*, surrounding)

*Professional military people are more comfortable in their own **ambience** than in the company of armchair soldiers.*

*Sundecks on ships have a pleasant **ambience** about them.*

Some diners go to expensive restaurants for the **ambience** as much as the food.

ambiguous—unclear, having more than one meaning (L *ambiguus*, from *ambigere*, to wander about, waver, from *ambi*, about, *agere*, to do)

*Cary Grant received an **ambiguous** telegram reading "How old Cary Grant?" Grant, known for his sense of humor, replied, "Old Cary Grant fine. How you?"*

The best antonym for **ambiguity** is clarity, a quality much to be desired in English composition.

ameliorate—to improve, make better (F *améliorer*, alter, L *melior*, better)

*The agency wished to **ameliorate** the condition of the refugees, but it was hampered by a lack of funds.*

ampersand—and, the symbol &, also called short *and*

> The **ampersand** *should be used only in company*
> *names.*

Every other use is tacky, but it's all right to use it once in a while in informal cursive writing. This symbol is taken from *and* plus *per se* (meaning by itself) plus *and*. Now you know why the shorthand symbol is used.

anachronistic—out of chronologic sequence (Gk *ana*, not, *chronos*, time)

> *Romance and historical novelists should be careful*
> *to avoid* **anachronistic** *events.*

In an episode of *Murder, She Wrote*, the obnoxious shock jock showed his ignorance by suggesting to Jessica Fletcher that she arrange an **anachronistic** conference with Dostoevsky about making a television series of *Crime and Punishment*.

ancillary—related, subordinate, complementary, auxiliary (L *ancilla*, maidservant)

> *Acoustics and design are* **ancillary** *to the study of*
> *architecture.*
> *Radiation is an* **ancillary** *treatment for certain kinds*
> *of cancer.*

android—automaton with human form, humanlike (Gk *andr*, man, *oeides*, oid, like)

> *Robots are the most* **android** *of all the automatons.*
> Star Trek *fans will remember Data, an endearing*
> **android**, *who was capable of human emotion.*

anesthesia—unconsciousness or state of no pain (Gk *an*, not, *asthesis*, feeling)

> *A new, experimental drug was used to induce* **anesthesia** *during the five-hour operation on the quarterback's knee.*

> Anesthetics, the agents or drugs used, should be distinguished from **anesthesia**.

antecedent—predecessor, ancestor (L *ante*, before, *cedere*, to go)

> *Americans point with pride to their* **antecedents**, *who immigrated to this country at great cost and sacrifice for political or economic freedom.*

> This word can also be used as an adjective:
> *Typewriters were* **antecedent** *to word processors.*
> *The verb should agree in number with its* **antecedent** *subject.*

arcane—mysterious, secret, concealed (L *arcanus*)

> *The film* Raiders of the Lost Ark *depicted the search for the* **arcane** *Holy Grail.*
> *Medieval alchemists were engaged in an* **arcane** *quest: to find the way to make gold from base metals.*

> Alchemists were also engaged in even more **arcane** pursuits: to find a panacea for all diseases and to discover a way to prolong life indefinitely.

argent—silver, silvery (L *argentum*)

> *The sea shone with an* **argent** *glow in the moonlight.*

*That day, the Aurora Borealis was **argent**, although in other climes Anouk had seen it in Technicolor.*

The explorer Sebastian Cabot may have given **Argentina** its name because of the beautiful silver jewelry and ornaments the inhabitants wore.

artifact—object made by humans, not a natural object (L *ars*, art, skill, *facere*, to make)

*The National Museum of Anthropology in Mexico City has fascinating collections of **artifacts** from Central American civilizations, including the Aztec and the Mayan.*

This word is also correctly spelled **artefact**.

asterisk—the symbol *, sometimes called star (Gk *asteriskos*, little star, *aster*, star)

Some day a jokester may come up with a song titled "Twinkle, Twinkle, Little Asterisk." But that would be redundant.

astronavigation—celestial navigation, "steering by the stars" (Gk *aster*, star, L *navis*, ship, *agere*, to lead, drive)

*Airplane pilots use **astronavigation** as well as instruments to steer by.*
*On Jan. 30, 1996, an amateur **astronomer** in Japan, Yuji Hayakutake, discovered a new comet, which was immediately named after him.*

The authority at the Fels Planetarium in Philadelphia tells me that Hayakutake is not the brightest comet in 440 years and not the closest in 440 years (there have been others), but taking both characteristics together, it is the brightest and the closest.

aural—relating to the ear or sound (L *auris*, ear)

> *Although some species of fish have no **aural** apparatus, they can sense motion or vibrations in the water, perhaps through some form of sonar.*

> This word sounds exactly like *oral*, which has to do with the mouth and not the ear, so the one word is often mistaken for the other.

auriferous—bearing or carrying gold (L *aurum*, gold, *iferous*, bearing)

> *The 1849 Gold Rush came soon after prospectors at Sutter's Mill found **auriferous** rocks.*
> *On Oscars night, a famous movie critic wisecracked that the starlet was downright **auriferous** but that the gold of her hair was spurious.*

austral—southern (L *australis*)

> *Exploring the **austral** seas was only for the bravest, because that part of the world was still uncharted.*
> *The smallest continent, **Australia**, which is an island as well, was so named because it is in the southern Pacific Ocean.*

avuncular—like an uncle (L *avunculus*, maternal uncle, the diminutive of *avus*, grandfather)

> *Milton Berle was called "Uncle Miltie" because of his sometimes **avuncular** air on his television show.*

B

bagatelle—a trifle, something of little consequence (F, from It *bagattella*)

> *For the Chief Executive Officer, one Mercedes was a mere bagatelle.*

A short piece of music or verse is often called a **bagatelle**. There is also a game called **bagatelle** that is similar to billiards.

barbaric—savage, uncivilized (Gk *barbaros*, foreigner)

> *Because of terrible means of destruction, modern wars are much more **barbaric** than those in bygone days.*
> *Stravinsky's ballet* Rite of Spring *caused a near-riot in Paris because of its unfamiliar **barbaric** rhythms and discords.*

A year later, audiences cheered Stravinsky's ballet and carried him out to the street on their shoulders "like a prizefighter," as a gendarme later said.

behemoth—monster (Heb *behemah*, beast)

> *The Trojan Horse, the **behemoth** brought to the gates of Troy by the Greeks, became a disastrous "gift" for the city's unfortunate inhabitants.*
> *With its far-flung empire, AT&T is one of the **behemoths** of the communications industry.*

*Baldwin locomotives, one of which is housed inside the Franklin Institute in Philadelphia, were called **behemoths** because of their immensity.*

belligerent—warlike, carrying on war, quarrelsome, argumentative (L *bellum*, war, *gerere*, to carry on, wage)

*Many have feared that the **belligerent** nations might take the world to the brink of war.*

*Jan's **belligerent** words provoked a confrontation.*

Other words from the same root are *antebellum* (before the war) and *bellicose* (combative).

bellwether—a sheep carrying a bell (ME, from *belle*, bell, *wether*, ram)

***Bellwethers** are used to lead or guide the flock into the meadow or the fold.*

*Bradburn, Inc. is the **bellwether** of the widget cartel.*

This word is sometimes misspelled "bellweather," but it has nothing to do with the weather.

bemused—dazed, sometimes bewitched or bothered as well, but always bewildered

*Effects of the confusing evidence could be seen in the **bemused** expressions of the jurors.*

Children at the circus are amused, not **bemused**, except perhaps by the magic antics of the clowns.

beneficence—goodness, kindness, favor, support, promotion (L *bene*, well, *facere*, to make, do)

Tragedies and misfortunes may cause some people to lose their faith in the inherent **beneficence** *of the human race.*

Mother Theresa's **beneficence** *is visible in her face.*

biennial—every two years, once in two years (L *bi*, two, *annum*, year)

The commission prepares for the state's **biennial** *sports competitions far in advance.*

Some crops are not profitable because they can be reaped only **biennially**.

Biennial should be carefully distinguished from *biannual*, which means twice a year; *semiannual* means every half-year or twice a year.

bigamous—relating to bigamy, the act of marrying one person while still being married to another (L *bi*, two, Gk *gamos*, marriage)

In Madama Butterfly, *Lieutenant Pinkerton enters into a* **bigamous** *marriage with his American fiancee.*

Polygamy (multiple marriages) has never been legal in the United States, and mere **bigamy** *is out too.*

biodegradable—capable of being destroyed by natural means (L *bio*, life, *gradus*, step, pace)

For the sake of the planet and for economic and public relations reasons, many manufacturers are using **biodegradable** *packing material rather than Styrofoam.*

blatant—obtrusive, noisy, offensive (unknown, but perhaps from L *blatire*, to gossip or chatter)

> *Blatant disregard of civility can result in senseless tragedies such as freeway shootings.*
> *The blatancy of Western culture is often lampooned in the foreign media.*

bovine—cowlike, patient, sluggish (LL *bovinus*, from L *bos*, ox, cow)

> *Ladd's bovine eyes were brown and unblinking.*
> *Jocelyn's bovine temperament was a great help in her research.*

broach—to introduce, announce, present (ME *brochen*, from OF *broche*)

> *Nature enthusiasts took the opportunity to broach the subject of a hike along the Appalachian trail.*

> Don't misspell this word "brooch," which means an ornamental pin.

buff—enthusiast, fan (probably from the buff coats worn around 1820 by volunteer firemen in New York City, who presumably were enthusiastic about putting out fires)

> *Theater buffs are delighted when their opinions coincide with those of the sometimes hypercritical critics.*
> *Carr's mystery plots are elaborate, and so they appeal only to true buffs like you and me.*

> The slang term "fan" is short for *fanatic*.

C

cacophony—unpleasant or discordant sound (Gk *cakos*, bad, *phonia*, sound)

> *He loved the city with all its* **cacophony**—*street sounds, noisy air-conditioners spewing cool air, the sudden screech of brakes.*

> *The unfamiliar* **cacophony** *of the katydids, owls, and other nocturnal creatures disturbed the city boy's sleep.*

> **Cacophony** is the antonym, the opposite, of *euphony*, which means good or pleasant sound.

caduceus—(ka-DOOS-ee-us) herald's wand, staff (L)

> ***Caducei*** *are favorite logos to denote swiftness, for example the winged staff with two serpents curled around it, used by the Medical Corps of the United States Air Force.*

> *Aesculapius, the Greco-Roman god of medicine, carried a different* **caduceus**, *a simple wooden staff with a forked top, with one serpent coiled around it.*

> The **caduceus** of Aesculapius became the official insignia (insigne is also correct) of the American Medical Association and the familiar symbol of the medical profession in general.

carcinogenic—causing or tending to cause cancer (NL, from *carcin*, cancer, *genic*, producing)

> *Many air pollutants, including industrial burnoff and tobacco smoke, are known to be* ***carcinogenic***.

> The constellation Cancer, portrayed in the Zodiac as a crab, lies between Leo and Gemini.

cardiology—the study and science of the heart and its diseases (Gk *kardia*, heart, *logos*, study, word, account)

> *An important subspecialty of internal medicine is* ***cardiology***.

carnivore—flesh-eater (L *carn*, flesh, *vorare*, to devour)

> *Animals are not the only* ***carnivores***; *insect-eating plants are also* ***carnivorous***.

cartographer—one who makes maps (F *carte*, map)

> *The Flemish geographer Gerhardus Mercator, who died in 1594, is perhaps the most famous* ***cartographer***.

> The Mercator "flat" projection is still seen in illustrations of old maps.

catharsis—purifying, cleansing, purging (Gk *katharsis*)

> *Confession of sins is often thought of as* ***catharsis*** *of the soul.*
> *Castor oil is an old household* ***cathartic*** *remedy.*

caustic—biting, acidic, corrosive (Gk *kaustikos*, burning)

> *Sulfuric acid is a **caustic** agent used in the laboratory to dissolve certain materials.*
>
> *Satirists use **caustic** humor to good advantage.*

Many Goldwynisms, solecisms attributed to Samuel Goldwyn, were never said by him, but they make for good anecdotes. His gag writers often teasingly attributed their own jokes to him. When a director told Goldwyn that a particular screen writer was too **caustic**, he is said to have replied, "Too **caustic**? The hell with it, we'll make the picture anyway."

Oscar Levant, a great performer of Gershwin music, was also noted for his **caustic** wit. He said about Doris Day's acting career that he "knew her before she was a virgin."

cerulean—deep blue, azure (L *caeruleus*)

> *The skies that autumn morning were a dazzling **cerulean**.*

charisma—an unusual quality of leadership (Gk)

> *President John F. Kennedy possessed **charisma**, and for the most part he used it well politically.*
>
> *Extraordinary teachers have the kind of **charisma** that inspires their students.*

This word is often mistakenly used to mean ordinary charm or persuasiveness. **Charisma** has a much stronger meaning, often having to do with leadership, and is much less common.

charlatan—quack, faker, fraud, pretender (It *ciarlatano*)

*In medical circles, **charlatans** who claim to be able to cure all diseases are called quacks.*

The German physician Franz Anton Mesmer, who practiced therapeutic hypnotism in Vienna, was thought to be a **charlatan** in his time, and he died in obscurity. Some researchers now believe that he was practicing psychosomatic medicine, an idea whose time had not yet come.

chauvinism—warmongering, unquestioning patriotism (F *chauvinisme*)

***Chauvinism** can blind its adherents to better, more rational ways to solve problems among nations than wars.*

Chauvin was a soldier whose life was fanatically dedicated to Napoleon. He even became a character in a play.

The usage of **chauvinism** has been extended to mean excessive partiality for any group, or just the opposite—extreme hostility toward members of the other sex in general.

chutzpah—nerve, gall, extreme self-confidence (Y, from Heb)

*The proverbial example of **chutzpah** is the man who kills his parents and then throws himself on the mercy of the court because he is an orphan.*

The Greek equivalent of **chutzpah** is *hubris*.

circadian—occurring daily or in about 24-hour cycles (L *circa*, about, *dies*, day)

> *"Morning persons" differ from night owls by virtue of different* **circadian** *rhythms.*

circuitous—roundabout, indirect (L *circuitus*, from *circum*, around, about, *ire*, to go)

> *The yellow brick road to Oz was so* **circuitous** *that Dorothy and her companions grew tired and frustrated.*
>
> *Politicians are particularly adept at speaking* **circuitously** *about crucial (and other) issues.*

claustrophobia—abnormal fear of being closed in (L *claustrum*, bar, bolt, lock, L and Gk, *phobia*, fear)

> *Patients may be so* **claustrophobic** *that they refuse to enter the narrow chamber used for computerized tomography.*
>
> *His* **claustrophobia** *in adult life was traced to painful episodes in his childhood, when he was locked in a closet all day for misbehaving.*

climax—highest point (L from Gk *klimax*, ladder)

> *For some Shakespeare enthusiasts, the play within a play is the* **climax** *of Hamlet.*
>
> *The American Revolution reached its* **climax** *when General Washington and his troops crossed the Delaware River and won the battle of Trenton.*

cogitation—reflection, thinking, meditation (L *cogitare*, from *co* + *agere*, to turn over in the mind)

*An occasional pause for **cogitation** refreshes the mind.*

*After much anxious **cogitation**, the pilot decided to land the single-engine plane on the freeway.*

comatose—in an unconscious or lethargic state (Gk *koma*, deep sleep)

*After the accident, Dr. Bancroft's patient was left in a **comatose** state, but seven years later she woke up, to the astonishment of her family and the entire medical group.*

*Speeches that go on too long can cause a **comatose** state and snores in the audience.*

compendium—short or abridged work, condensation of a larger work (L, shortcut)

Reader's Digest *is a **compendium** of book excerpts and articles of general interest.*

This word is mistakenly used to mean a large, capacious work. It means quite the opposite.

complacency—undue self-satisfaction, smugness (L *com*, *placere*, to please)

***Complacent** players lose baseball games—and football games—and tennis tournaments.*

*Displeased with the **complacency** of the school district, the parents held a town meeting to change its priorities.*

complaisant—eager to please (MF *complaire*, to acquiesce, L *complacere*, to please greatly)

> *Middle-level executives were too **complaisant** for the feisty new president, who openly labeled them "yes-men."*

contretemps—embarrassing or dangerous situation (F, *contre*, counter, *temps*, time)

> *Khrushchev, one of the main players in this **contretemps** at the United Nations, banged his shoe on the desk in a rage.*
>
> *Mistranslation of a Russian phrase caused a **contretemps** that led to some unfortunate decisions. Gorbachev had warned the United States to "take heed," but it was mistranslated as "take care," a clear threat.*

KON-tra-tawn is the best English pronunciation I can offer, as the word is pronounced through the nose.

convoluted—curved, tortuous, coiled (L *com*, with, *volvere*, to enfold)

> *The human brain is so **convoluted** that it presents difficult choices for neurosurgeons; they sometimes operate on patients who have life-threatening disorders.*
>
> ***Convoluted** events call for unconvoluted solutions, but these are seldom achieved.*

By extension this word means *complicated*.

corporeal—relating to a physical body, material (L *corpus*, body)

> *Religious institutions tend to be concerned more with spiritual concerns than **corporeal** ones.*

corrigendum—error to be corrected (L *corrigere*, to correct)

>*Acknowledging her mistake, the researcher agreed to have a **corrigendum** appear in the next issue of the journal.*
>
>*Most newspapers print **corrigenda** in the same section where the original errors appeared.*

cosmopolitan—having a world view, worldly (Gk *kosmos, polites*, citizen)

>*People who travel a great deal tend to be more **cosmopolitan** than stay-at-homes.*
>
>*The isolationist always finds himself at odds with the **cosmopolitan**.*

coup de grace—(koo-di-grahs) blow of mercy (F)

>*In medieval times, a dagger called a misericord was used to administer the **coup de grace** to a criminal.*
>
>Warriors sometimes used a misericord to end a comrade's suffering. Another *coup de grace* is the final, single shot of a firing squad.
>
>*Terminally ill because of poor management, the Bireme Company received the **coup de grace** from the bankruptcy court.*

covert—concealed, hidden (F *couvrir*, to cover, L *coopertus*, covered)

>*It is no secret that almost every country in the world has spies conducting **covert** operations.*
>
>The opposite of **covert** is *overt*.

craven—cowardly, fainthearted (from ME *cravant*, cowardly)

> *Bert Lahr's most famous role was as the **craven** lion in* The Wizard of Oz.
> *Running away from an unfair fight is not **craven**.*

credible—believable (L *credere*, to believe)

> *Jurors thought the witnesses were **credible**, and acquitted the defendant.*

> The opposite of **credible** is *incredible*, unbelievable.
> Don't confuse **credible** with *creditable*, which means worthy or respectable.

criterion—standard, standard of reference (Gk)

> *Integrity is one important **criterion** by which people are judged.*
> *Speed and maneuverability are **criteria** used to classify Air Force jets.*

cryogenics—science of freezing (Gk *krymos*, icy cold, ISV *genic*, producing, forming)

> *The aerospace industry uses **cryogenics** extensively, and so do frozen-food companies.*
> *Researchers use **cryogenics** in their study of human tissues.*

cryptic—puzzling, hidden, secret (Gk *kryptos*)

> *Computer manuals are often **cryptic** to the average user.*

43

*The Oracle at Delphi gave such **cryptic** answers that the hearers could interpret them any way they wished.*

In the Oedipus legend of Greek mythology, the Sphinx at Thebes was the destroyer sent by the gods to kill all passersby who could not solve the **cryptic** riddle: "What walks on four feet in the morning, on two at noon, and on three in the evening?" The only one to solve the riddle was Orestes, who answered: "Man crawls on all fours as a baby, walks upright in the prime of life, and uses a staff in old age." The Sphinx then killed herself.

culpable—guilty, blameworthy (L *culpare*, to blame)

*The public's verdict was that those who witnessed the hold-up and stood by silently were as **culpable** as the perpetrators.*

cyberspace—the universe of computers and the networks that link them (from Gk *kybernetes*, steersman, governor)

*Meeting in **cyberspace** can be exciting and productive, but beware the frauds and malefactors who also have access to it.*

D

dearth—lack, scarcity (ME *derthe*, from *dere*, costly, dear)

*The **dearth** of rainfall in 1992 left the reservoir too low in water and full of sediment.*

debacle—collapse, downfall (F *débâcler*, to unbolt, unbar)

> *The fateful year 1929 saw a **debacle** on Wall Street that ruined millions of investors and caused banks all over the United States to fail.*

decimate—to destroy, injure or damage to an extreme (L *decimus*, tenth, from *decem*, ten)

> *In former times, to **decimate** was to kill every tenth man, especially in a military sense.*

> Nowadays, **decimate** is used too loosely to indicate an injury of a somewhat serious kind.

deleterious—hurtful, harmful (Gk *deleterios*)

> *Dietitians tell us that too much fat in the diet may cause **deleterious** plaques in the blood vessels.*
> *Acid rain is **deleterious** to our cities' statues and other monuments.*

demography—statistical and sociologic science and study of human populations and subpopulations (F *démographie*, from Gk *demos*, population, people, *graphos*, written)

> ***Demography** is a fascinating field for workers talented in mathematics and interested in populations.*

> **Demographers** can tell us how many people live in the United States, where they work, how they study and are educated, what percentage of drivers use a certain kind of gasoline, the number of buyers of cereals or other grocery products, and thousands of other valuable facts.

Demographers are employed by business, industry, organizations, and governing bodies, to name just a few. They are indispensable to the federal government and the Congress, which base many expenditures on **demographers'** statistics.

deprecate—to disapprove, frown on (L *deprecari*, to avert by prayer)

> *Don't be too quick to **deprecate** other people's beliefs.*

derogatory—disparaging, detracting (L *derogatus*)

> *Their parents wisely made no **derogatory** remarks about the children's behavior in public, and saved their criticism until they all got home.*

deterrent—discouragement, restraint (L *deterrere*, to deter)

> *Capital punishment has been abolished in some countries, because they do not believe it is a **deterrent** to crime.*

digitize—to put into digital form (L *digitus*, finger, toe, digit)

> *A scanner **digitizes** drawings or photographs so that you can edit them on your computer.*
> ***Digitizing** is a necessity for people who want to apply for certain computer positions at this plant.*

dilettante—connoisseur, amateur enthusiast, dabbler (It *dilettante*, from *dilettare*, from L *delectare*, to delight)

> *As a connoisseur of the arts, she was superb. As a painter, she was a **dilettante**.*

This word can mean either amateurish or expert. Art critics are careful to use the right words in describing artists or would-be artists.

dismal—unpleasant, evil, unlucky, disagreeable (ME, from ML *dies*, day, *mali*, evil, bad)

Medieval calendar makers considered two days in each month, 24 in a year, to be **dismal***, that is, unlucky.*

The greatest expectations sometimes have **dismal** *results.*

The ancient Romans had a similar designation, the ides, a period between the 13th and 15th of the month. Julius Caesar was warned to beware the ides of March—with good reason, for it was during one of those **dismal** days that he was assassinated.

disparate—different, unequal, unlike (L *disparare*, to separate, from *disparatus*, from *parare*, to prepare)

Singapore is an island with three **disparate** *cultures, Chinese, Malay and Indian.*

English is one of the official languages, along with Chinese, Malay and Tamil.

Joanne Woodward won an Academy Award for her portrayal in 1957 of a woman with **disparate** *personalities (The Three Faces of Eve).*

You will recognize the root *parare* in the motto of the United States Coast Guard: "Semper Paratus," "Always Prepared."

disseminate—spread about, make widespread (L *disseminatus*, from *dis*, apart, *semen*, seed)

> *The town crier, ringing his bell in the center of the common, would shout "Hear ye! Hear ye!" and* **disseminate** *the latest news three times each day except Sunday.*

diurnal—daily, occurring every day (L *diurnalis*)

> *The earth's rotation is a* **diurnal** *motion.*
> *Everyone needs a respite from* **diurnal** *duties.*

dolorous—sad, painful, regrettable (L *dolor*, pain)

> *Her extravagance was born of deprivation in the* **dolorous** *days of the Great Depression.*

downtime—unproductive period

> *Factory workers can ill afford a* **downtime**.
> *The Chief Financial Officer complained that there were too many* **downtimes** *in the factory's computer division.*

draconian—extremely severe or harsh

> *The original boycott was brought on by the* **draconian** *measures of tax collectors.*

Sometimes this word is correctly capitalized, since it originates with Draco, an Athenian legislator, who lived about 621 BC, and was noted for his severe code of laws.

The term *boycott* stems from Charles Boycott, an English land agent in Ireland, who refused to reduce rents and was forever after ostracized.

dyslexia—a disturbance of the ability to read (NL, from *dys*, difficult, abnormal, from Gk *lexis*, word)

***Dyslexia** did not prevent these diligent students from completing their education.*

*Some of the world's foremost achievers, such as Leonardo da Vinci and Thomas A. Edison, have been **dyslexic**.*

E

ebullient—bubbly, exuberant, enthusiastic (L *bullire*, to bubble)

*Barbara Walters' **ebullient** personality serves her well as a television interviewer.*

*Old Faithful has an **ebullient** energy that can be seen several times a day.*

eclectic—selective, having many different sources (Gk *eklegein*, to pick out, select)

*One **eclectic** branch of psychiatry blends the principles of Freud, Jung and Adler, as well as more current theorists.*

*Taste in music can be **eclectic** without being either stuffy or vulgar.*

McGuffy's readers were called **eclectic** because they stressed the "three R's," readin', writin' and 'rithmetic.

effervescent—bubbly, exuberant (L *effervescere*, to begin to boil)

> *Even as a child, Beverly Sills was so **effervescent** that she was nicknamed "Bubbles."*
> *Speedy Alka-Seltzer was an animated character advertising the **effervescent** antacid tablets.*

effete—used up, exhausted, outdated (L *ex*, out, *fetus*, fruitful)

> *Snobbishness is a hallmark of **effete** social climbers.*
> *In her novels, Jane Austen skillfully and elegantly portrays the **effeteness** of late-18th-century gentility.*

egalitarian—believing in equality (F *égalité*, equality, L *aequalitas*, equality)

> *The avowed objective of the French revolutionists was **egalitarianism**, and on July 14, 1789, they led thousands of Parisians in storming the Bastille to free political prisoners.*

egregious—flagrant, outrageous, notorious, in conspicuous bad taste (L *e*, out of, *grex*, herd, flock)

> *The House of Lords was outraged by the member's **egregious** tirade against the Prime Minister.*

*Even experts make **egregious** errors in every field of human endeavor.*

As Fiorello La Guardia once said, "When I make a mistake it's a beaut!"

elusive—fleeting, evasive, baffling (L *eludere*, to elude)

*Agatha Christie's **elusive** perpetrators were pursued relentlessly by the immortal Belgian sleuth, Hercule Poirot.*
*James Joyce's meanings are **elusive** to all but a few scholars who have devoted years of study to his idiosyncratic novels.*

empathy—the capacity for associating with someone else's feelings (translation from G *einfühlung*)

*A person who has **empathy** can put himself or herself in another person's shoes, even without having gone through the same experience.*

encomium—praise (L, from Gk *enkomion*, a laudatory poem)

*The highest **encomium** came from a fellow Nobel Laureate.*

endemic—native, indigenous, confined to a particular region (Gk *endemos*, from *en*, in, *demos*, populace)

*Medicinal herbs are **endemic** in the rain forests.*
*Because of the ease of worldwide transportation, especially by jet plane, few diseases are **endemic**.*

enervate—to take energy or vigor away (L *e*, out of, *nervus*, nerve)

> *Corruption has **enervated** many a metropolitan police force.*
>
> *Discouragement can **enervate** the most courageous.*

> This word is sometimes mistakenly taken to mean energize. It means the opposite.

ennui—(ahn-wee) boredom, weariness, dissatisfaction (OF *enui*, annoyance)

> *Yawning, a conspicuous sign of **ennui**, is a sign that the lecturer should cut it short.*

entomology—scientific study of insects (F, from Gk, from *e*, out, *temnein*, to cut)

> *The word **entomology**, a zoologic term meaning the study of insects, is often facetiously used instead of* etymology, *the study of words.*

ephemeral—temporary, fleeting, transient (Gk *ephemeros*, lasting a day, from *epi*, upon, on, *hemera*, a day)

> *The popularity of many works of art is as **ephemeral** as the morning dew.*
>
> *News on the electronic media is **ephemeral**, but the printed word lasts indefinitely.*
>
> *Napoleon's rule of France was **ephemeral**, lasting only 100 days.*

Alfred Kahn, a professor of economics but undoubtedly also a philosopher, wrote that life is just a concatenation of **ephemeralities**.

epicenter—center, focus of an earthquake (L, from Gk *epi*, on, L *centrum*, center)

Anchorage, Alaska, was the **epicenter** *of a 1964 earthquake that registered 8.4 on the Richter scale.*

Boston, which playfully claims for its nickname the Hub of the Universe, is the **epicenter** *of culture and medicine in New England.*

epigram—terse, witty, pithy or wise saying (Gk *epi*, on, *graphein*, to write)

Benjamin Franklin's Poor Richard's Almanack *was full of* **epigrams** *that are still quoted extensively.*

Why "Poor Richard"? Franklin sometimes used the pseudonym or *nom de plume* Richard Saunders.

epitome—summary, abridgment, apex, acme, embodiment (Gk *epi*, upon, *temnein*, to cut)

A short or condensed work is an **epitome** *of a larger one.*

Beau Brummell was the **epitome** *of London sartorial splendor.*

epizootic—epidemic among animals (Gk *epi*, on, *zoion*, animal)

"Mad cow" disease was **epizootic** *in Great Britain in early 1996.*

ergo—therefore, hence (OL *e* + *rogo*, from the direction of)

> *California is the most populous state in the union;* ***ergo*** *it has the greatest number of representatives in the Congress.*
>
> *"Humana sum;* ***ergo*** *erro." "I am human; therefore I err."*
>
> *"Cogito* ***ergo*** *sum." "I think, therefore I am" (René Descartes).*

erratum—error (L)

> *Even the best dictionary can contain an* ***erratum****, which may be corrected in a subsequent edition.*
>
> The plural is **errata**. A word related in meaning is *corrigendum*, which means something to be corrected.

esoteric—difficult to understand, mysterious (Gk *esoterikos*)

> *The tax laws are so* ***esoteric*** *that most of us need accountants to prepare our returns.*
>
> Rhyming slang used by Cockneys in London is too **esoteric** for outsiders. Here are some examples: "mince pies" for *eyes*, "trouble and strife" for *wife*, "apples and pears" for *stairs* and "half-inch" for *pinch*.

esthetics—philosophy or science of beauty, art, and taste (Gk *aesthetikos*, of sense perception)

> ***Esthetics*** *embraces painting, sculpture, decoration, music and all the other arts.*

*Dr. Albert Barnes, who assembled a splendid collection of Impressionist paintings in the early 1900s, was a keen student of **esthetics**.*

This word is also correctly spelled **aesthetics**.

estivate—to pass the summer in one place (L *aestivare*, to spend the summer)

*Summer visitors to Maryland's Eastern Shore tend to **estivate** in a state of relaxation bordering on torpor.*

To *hibernate* is to spend the winter in one place in a state of inactivity or lethargy.

etymology—science and study of the origins of words (L *etymologia*, from Gk *etymon*, the literal meaning of a word according to its origin, from *etymos*, true)

*Knowing the **etymology** of a word can help in understanding its meaning.*
***Etymologists** study the evolution, origins and interrelation of languages.*

eugenics—science dealing with improvement of human qualities (Gk *eu*, good, well, *genes*, born)

*Geneticists have made great strides not only in mapping genes but in **eugenics**, that is, in improving inheritable characteristics.*

More has been discovered about chromosomes and genes in the last 50 years than in the entire previous history of science.

eulogy—praise, speech in praise (Gk *eu*, good, well, *logia*, logy)

> *It is customary in some countries to have a relative deliver the **eulogy** at the funeral of a family member.*
> *The speech introducing the day's moderator was a **eulogy** in itself.*

euphonious—sounding good (Gk *eu*, good, sweet, *phonos*, sound)

> *The whistles, cheers and laughter of the crowd were always **euphonious** to the Harlem Globetrotters.*

> The antonym, the opposite, of **euphony** is *cacophony* (bad sound).

euphoria—feeling good (Gk *eu*, good, well, *phoros*, carrying, bearing, tendency)

> *Writing a good composition brings about a well-deserved and gratifying **euphoria**.*
> *Being on cloud nine is being **euphoric**.*

exculpate—vindicate, to clear of blame (L *ex*, out, *culpare*, to blame)

> *A P.I. (private investigator) was hired to find evidence that would **exculpate** the defendant.*
> ***Exculpatory** information must be brought to the attention of both prosecution and defense.*

extrapolate—extend, expand (L *extra*, out, E *polate*)

> *Pharmacologists cannot necessarily **extrapolate** the effects of drugs in animals to their effects in humans.*

*The world population in particular years beyond the year 2000 can be **extrapolated** from current statistics.*

extraterrestrial—outside the earth (L *extra*, outside, *terra*, earth, world)

*Satellites in outer space are constantly searching for intelligible **extraterrestrial** sounds.*
The film E.T. *tells the touching story of an **extraterrestrial** being and its friendship with a compassionate human boy.*

extrovert—outgoing person (L *extra*, out, *vertere*, to turn)

*An **extrovert** can be the life of the party or just a nuisance who cavorts around the room with a lampshade on his head.*

This word is also correctly spelled **extravert**.

F

fauna—animals, animal life (L *faunus*, faun)

*Zoologists all over the world go to the Serengeti National Park in Tanzania to study its magnificent **fauna**.*

The phrase "flora and fauna" often refers to the plant life (flora) and the animal life (fauna) of a particular region.

faux pas—misstep, social blunder, error (F, false step)

> *Leaving a party without saying goodbye to the hosts is a **faux pas**.*
> *"Oops" is a sometimes acceptable apology for a mild **faux pas**.*

This French phrase, which has passed painlessly into our language, is pronounced *foh-pah*, not *fox-pass*.

ferrous—iron-bearing, containing iron (L *ferrum*, iron, *ous*, having, being full of)

> *Construction contractors use **ferrous** products extensively, especially those made of steel.*

fiat—edict, command (L, let it be done, from *fieri*, to become)

> *Tolerance and equality can never be achieved solely by **fiat**.*
> *The conscience has its own **fiats**.*

filial—relating to a son or daughter (L *filius*, son)

> *In the field of Chinese ethics, **filial** piety, children's reverence for parents, is considered the paramount virtue and the basis for all moral human relations.*
> *Although she was only a niece, Ashley had a **filial** love for her Aunt Bess.*

flagrant—notorious, glaring, conspicuous (L *flagrare*, to burn)

> ***Flagrant** disregard of civility and reasoned thinking led to a rash of frivolous lawsuits.*

*The nuclear-power plant engineer was adjudged guilty of a **flagrant** dereliction of duty after he was discovered asleep at his monitoring post.*

flora—plants, flowers, foliage, usually of a region (L)

*Spectacular displays of **flora** can be enjoyed at Longwood Gardens in Kennett Square, Pennsylvania.*

Strangely enough, the bacteria residing in the intestine are called **flora**.

foible—weak point, flaw, shortcoming, failing (F *faible*, weak)

*P. G. Wodehouse wrote humorous novels about the **foibles** of the idle, but lovable, rich.*

In French, the *faible* is the part of a sword blade from the middle to the point, and therefore the weaker part.

You can see where our word *feeble* originates.

formication—feeling of insects creeping on oneself (L *formica*, ant)

*All during the journey through the thick undergrowth, she had a dreadful feeling of **formication**, although the pests could not be seen.*

forte—(fort) strong point (MF, strong)

*Judy won the national bee, because spelling is her **forte**.*

The *forte* of a sword is the strong part, from the middle to the hilt.

The Italian *forte* means loud, and is pronounced in two syllables, unlike the French word.

fragile—delicate, frail, tenuous, weak (MF, from L *fragilis*)

> *Their confidence is based on a **fragile** foundation.*
>
> *Most perennial plants are too **fragile** to withstand the harsh Eastern winters, but they bloom again in the spring.*

frenetic—frenzied, frantic, hectic (Gk *phrenitikos*, inflammation of the brain, from *phren*, mind)

> ***Frenetic** activity was seen throughout the museum before the opening of the opulent Faberge exhibition.*
>
> *The **frenetic** screams of the Grateful Dead fans could be heard even outside the stadium.*

G

gaffe—mistake, faux pas (F)

> *The most conspicuous **gaffes** made in newspapers are factual errors.*
>
> *Knowing the tight deadlines, careful readers usually forgive the typographic **gaffes**.*

gambit—opening move, a chess opening in which a piece is sacrificed for later advantage (It *gambetto*, gambit, tripping up, from *gamba*, leg)

> *The aerospace company's **gambit** eventually paid off for the major stockholders, who had wisely held on to their shares.*
>
> *Operation Overlord, which began on D-Day with the storming of the Normandy coast, was the supreme **gambit** of the Allies.*

garrulous—talkative (L *garrulus*, from *garrire*, to chatter)

> *Norman Rockwell loved to paint the **garrulous** characters he saw sitting around the cracker barrel swapping lies.*
>
> Synonyms for **garrulous** are *verbose, prolix, wordy, chatty* and *loquacious*.

genealogy—history of ancestry (Gk *genea*, race, family, *logia*, logy, study)

> *It is said that many American presidents could trace their **genealogies** to the kings and nobles of England.*
>
> *The Mayflower would have sunk outside Southampton harbor if all the people who now claim **genealogy** back to it had actually been on it.*

generic—general, not specific, not individual, not proprietary, characteristic of a group (F *générique*, from L *genus*, class, group, kind)

> ***Generic** drugs are over-the-counter (OTC) products.*
>
> *By design, the Rockettes have a **generic** look.*

Trademarked or proprietary drugs, the opposite of **generic** drugs, are patented by their manufacturers for a finite term.

genuflect—to bend the knee, to be servile or humble (L *genu*, knee, *flectere*, to bend)

> *The mavericks who refused to **genuflect** before their political masters were drummed out of the party.*
> *Wedding pictures show the royal couple **genuflecting** before the Archbishop of Canterbury.*

geriatric—relating to old age (Gk *geras*, old age, E *atric*)

> *In the United States the **geriatric** population is growing at a faster rate than any other group, a process called the "graying of America."*

germane—relevant, pertinent (ME, MF *germain*, having the same parents)

> *Angry words are seldom **germane** to the subject in contention.*
> *Economic issues are always **germane** to social or political issues.*

glitch—slip, misstep, mistake, malfunction (probably from G *glitschen*, to slip, slide)

> *A faulty cotter pin caused a **glitch** in the satellite's liftoff.*
> *There's many a **glitch** 'twixt the cup and the lip.*

Gordian—pertaining to something seemingly insoluble, an extreme difficulty (from Gk *Gordios*)

> *To cut the **Gordian** knot is to solve a seemingly insoluble problem with a brilliant stroke.*

Gordius, the mythologic founder of Phrygia, tied a knot in a chariot thong that could be unraveled only by someone proclaimed by the oracle to become the ruler of Asia. All who had come to that place failed in the attempt, but Alexander the Great simply cut the Gordian knot with one blow of his sword.

This word is also spelled with a lowercase *g*.

gratuitous—given freely, unnecessary, groundless, not called for by the circumstances (L *gratus*, pleasing, grateful)

> *Harsh criticism is usually **gratuitous**.*
> *Don Rickles is famous for his **gratuitous** insults of celebrities.*

A generous tip or **gratuity** is gladly given for services above and beyond the call of duty.

gravamen—burden, material part or basis (L *gravis*, heavy)

> *The **gravamen** of the Bill of Complaint was negligence on the houseowner's part to keep the sidewalk clear of snow.*

gravitate—go in the direction of (L *gravitas*, weight)

> *The younger children **gravitated** to others of the same age.*

*Their conversations at the dinner table inevitably and disastrously **gravitated** toward religion and politics.*

gregarious—social, sociable (L *gregarius*, from *grex*, herd, flock)

*Human beings create cities because we are **gregarious** by nature.*

Spinoffs of this word include *aggregate* and *congregate* (to come together), and *segregate* (*separate*).

gremlin—mischievous imp, bad influence (origin unknown)

***Gremlins** were loose in the hangar that day, with mechanics dropping tools on coworkers' toes and oil being spattered on walls and floors.*

grist—grain for grinding (OE *grist*)

*Every experience, every conversation was **grist** for Studs Terkel's mill, and he used them skillfully in his books.*

H

hagiography—study or biography of saints (Gk *hagios*, holy, saints, *graphein*, to write)

*St. Augustine is a prominent name found in every **hagiography**.*

Hagia Sophia (Gk, holy wisdom), Santa Sophia, was originally a Christian church in Constantinople (now Istanbul). It became a mosque in 1453. The present edifice, itself a masterpiece of Byzantine architecture and an art museum, was built in 532-537 by Emperor Justinian.

hedonist—someone who lives for pleasure (Gk *hedone*, pleasure)

> *Life on the Riviera was ideal for the **hedonist**.*
> *The reckless pursuit of **hedonism** led to the billionaire's downfall.*

herbivorous—grass- or plant-eating (L *herba*, grass, *vorare*, to devour)

> *Giraffes and giant pandas are **herbivorous**.*
>
> So are vegetarians.

Herculean—strong, of giant proportions, of great difficulty (from Hercules)

> *Designing the space shuttle Endeavor was a **Herculean** task for the aerospace engineers.*

Hercules (L, from Gk Herakles), a hero in Greco-Roman mythology, possessed great strength and accomplished tasks that were impossible for anyone else.

In 1984 Arnold Schwarzenegger played the villainous, homicidal Terminator, but later films cast him in a better light as Hollywood's Action Hero of Choice, the **Hercules** of Hollywood.

hibernate—to be dormant or lethargic during the winter (L *hibernus*, of winter, wintry)

> *Bears are not the only creatures that **hibernate**; icy streets and storms cause humans in harsh climates to **hibernate** also.*

> To *estivate* is to be dormant or lethargic during the summer months.

hirsute—hairy, shaggy (L *hirsutus*)

> *In the movie* Planet of the Apes, *written by Rod Serling, the **hirsute** apes are the sympathetic masters and humans their savage subjects.*

holistic—emphasizing the relationship between parts and wholes (Gk *holos*, complete, entire)

> ***Holistic** medicine treats the patient in his or her entirety rather than as a bearer of disease.*

homily—lecture, discourse (Gk *homilos*, crowd, assembly)

> *The pope delivered a **homily** called "Urbis et Orbis," "to the city and the world," in which he pleaded for peace in troubled or warring countries.*

homogeneous—of the same or similar kind, equivalent (Gk *homogenes*, from *homo*, the same, *genos*, race, kind)

> *Japan has one of the most **homogeneous** populations in the world.*

Mormons, members of the Church of Latter-Day Saints, tend toward **homogeneity** *in their ethics, principles and beliefs.*

homograph—the same word, or spelled the same but meaning different things (Gk *homo*, same, *graphos*, written)

Invalid *and* invalid *are* **homographs***. One means an ill person; the other, something null and void.*

Invalid, an ill person, is accented on the first syllable. **Invalid**, describing a nullity, is accented on the second syllable.

The French comic dramatist Moliere cast himself in his own play, *The Imaginary* **Invalid** (*Le Malade Imaginaire*), but collapsed from a severe hemorrhage during a performance and died the same day.

Homographs can also mean words that are spelled the same but mean completely *opposite* things.

Cleave means to separate or to cling together.

Apparent can mean seemingly evident or clearly evident, readily perceptible.

To *sanction* means to approve or to punish.

Also see *homonym* and *homophone*.

homonym—words spelled the same and sometimes with the same pronunciation, but meaning different things (Gk *homonymos*, having the same name)

Lean *means slim or thin; to lean means to depend. They are* **homonyms***.*

Homonym and **homophone** are ordinarily used synonymously and interchangeably, since there is only a slight difference between them.

Also see *homograph* and *homophone*.

homophone—words with the same pronunciation but spelled differently and meaning different things (Gk *homo*, same, *phonos*, sound)

Write, right *and* rite *are* **homophones**, *that is, they all sound the same but mean completely different things.*

Also see *homograph* and *homonym*.

honorific—expressing honor or respect (L *honorare*)

Sports writers conferred the **honorific** *"Sultan of Swat" on Babe Ruth. He was major-league baseball's home run king, with 714, until Hank Aaron eclipsed his record in 1974 and finished with 755.*

Oliver Wendell Holmes, Jr., a justice of the United States Supreme Court, was given the **honorific** *"The Great Dissenter" because of his well-considered and elegantly written dissenting opinions.*

horology—the science of measuring time, the art of constructing timepieces (Gk *hora*, period of time, time of day, *logy*, study)

The sundial, an early product of **horology**, *can still be seen in some gardens.*

Horologists *construct grandfather clocks that show not only the hour but the phases of the moon.*

hortatory—urging, attempting to persuade, advisory (L *hortatus*)

> *The candidate's speech was more **hortatory** than enlightening.*

> The word *exhortation* comes from the same root.

hubris—gall, nerve, arrogance, excessive self-confidence (Gk *hybris*)

> *Celebrities who refuse to give autographs under any circumstances are guilty of **hubris**.*
> *Mussolini manifested all the **hubris** of power.*

> You may never see or use the word *sophrosyne*, which is the opposite of **hubris**. It means temperance, prudence or self-control.

hyperbole—gross exaggeration (Gk *hyperbole*, excess, extravagant)

> ***Hyperbole** is saying, "If I've told you once I've told you a thousand times."*
> ***Hyperbole** is the last refuge of the linguistically insecure.*

> The shortened form **hype** is used extensively in describing movies and television series.

hypercritical—overly critical, faultfinding in trivial matters (Gk *hyper*, over, above, *kritike*, criticism)

> *Those who care for children should never be **hypercritical**, for harsh words may ring forever in a child's mind.*

hypothermia—abnormally low body temperature (Gk *hypo,* under, beneath, *therme,* heat)

> *Dramatic pictures of the boy's rescue from the icy pond were seen on the evening television news. He had been under water for 20 minutes and was suffering from severe **hypothermia**.*

I

icon—image, idol (Gk *eikon,* resembling)

> *The Hermitage, a museum in St. Petersburg, Russia, contains innumerable **icons** of saints.*
> *Although they were British, the Beatles became an American **icon**.*
> *A Wall of Fame in the restaurant bears the caricatures of local sports **icons.***

Icon is also used in computer language to denote a small picture or graphic representation—on the screen of a program, file or function—that the user can choose. The **icon**, which is usually in a box, can be called up by clicking a mouse.

idiosyncrasy—a characteristic peculiar to one entity or person, eccentricity (Gk *idio,* personal, distinct, personal, individual, *synkrasis,* mixing, blending)

> *Her refusal to make left turns into streets was only one of her driving **idiosyncrasies**.*

A small group of subjects reported **idiosyncratic** *reactions to the investigational drug.*

One eccentric businessman in Boston never paid any attention to the one-hour difference during Daylight Saving Time. His clients were forced to bow to this **idiosyncrasy**, and his friends forgave it.

illicit—unlawful (L *in*, not, *licitus*, lawful)

Some characters in the opera Carmen *were engaged in an* **illicit** *activity, smuggling.*
Evidence obtained by **illicit** *means is tainted, and therefore inadmissible in court.*

illuminate—to light up, enlighten (L *in*, into, *lumen*, light)

Backlighting was used to **illuminate** *the stained-glass rose windows of the cathedral.*
St. Gregory the **Illuminator** *(240-332 AD) was the founder and patron saint of the Armenian church.*
Floodlights **illuminated** *the Field of Dreams, and the fans came.*

impecunious—poor, penniless (L *im*, not, *pecunia*, money)

Dickens wrote about people who were **impecunious** *but nonetheless rich in character and compassion.*

impervious—impenetrable, not open (L *im*, not, *pervius*, from *per*, through, *via*, road, way)

Police officers often wear vests that are **impervious** *to most kinds of bullets.*

*Lord Worcester's haughty manner gave the impression that he was **impervious** to insults.*

incredible—unbelievable, unlikely, improbable (L *in*, not, *credere*, to believe)

*Marco Polo's tales of riches and spices in far-off lands were **incredible** at first to his fellow Venetians.*

Bystanders in a Texas town looked on *incredulously* as cowboys rounded up cattle that had escaped from an overturned trailer truck. These words should be differentiated: Things are **incredible**; people are *incredulous*.

indigenous—native, originating in that region (L *indigena*, native)

*Corn is **indigenous** to the United States.*

*Digitalis, an herb **indigenous** to Eurasian countries, is used as a cardiac stimulant.*

infinitesimal—tiny, almost zero (NL *infinitesimus*, infinite in rank, from L *infinitus*, infinite)

*Differences between identical twins are **infinitesimal**.*

*In building bridges, or other massive engineering work, even an **infinitesimal** error can have disastrous results.*

Constructors of the 180-foot-high campanile nicknamed the Leaning Tower of Pisa made a seemingly **infinitesimal** error by building on a foundation only about 10 feet deep. Today the tower is almost 17 feet out of perpendicular.

iniquity—wrongful conduct, sin, wickedness (L *in*, not, *aequus*, unjust, unequal)

> *Communities work with the legal system in trying to remedy the **iniquity** of child abuse.*
> *What is **iniquity** to fundamentalists may simply be a difference of opinion.*

You should be careful to distinguish this word from **inequity** by pronouncing each carefully. An **iniquity** is more serious than an inequity, for example an inequity in wages, although that may be a sin, too.

innuendo—insinuation, hint (L *innuere*, to hint)

> *Gossip columnists and certain television personalities use **innuendo** to titillate their audiences.*
> *To paraphrase an adage attributed to the 19th-century Baptist preacher C. H. Spurgeon, **innuendo** (a lie, in the original) travels round the world while truth is putting her boots on.*

insouciant—(in-soos-ee-ant) indifferent, nonchalant, without a care (F *insoucier*, from *in*, not, *soucier*, to disturb, trouble, from L *sollicitare*, to disturb, agitate)

> *Eustace Tilley, the splendidly dressed man on the annual cover of* The New Yorker *magazine, has an **insouciant** air about him, because he is ignoring a butterfly flitting around his head.*

interregnum—lapse, period between two regimes (L *inter*, between, *regnum*, dominion)

> *Anne of Austria was chosen regent for the* ***interregnum*** *between the king's death and the dauphin's accession to the throne, but Cardinal Mazarin held the real power.*
>
> *Lame-duck congresspeople are always the victims of the* ***interregnum*** *between election and inauguration.*

intransigent—uncompromising, unshakable, immovable (Sp *intransigente*, from L *in*, not, *transiger*, to compromise)

> *The Stamp Act of 1765 aroused the fury of the American colonists. The British parliament reversed its* ***intransigent*** *stand and repealed the act only a year later.*

Businessmen, lawyers, journalists and merchants vehemently opposed the Act, which levied a tax on all papers, newspapers, journals, legal documents, and advertisements issued in the American colonies. Because the colonists were not represented in Parliament, they condemned the Act as taxation without representation.

introvert—one turned inward toward oneself (L *intro*, within, toward, *vertere*, to turn)

> *Poets and other writers are often more* ***introverted*** *than nonwriters, perhaps because of the solitary nature of the writing process.*

Introverts are often called wallflowers. Their opposites are *extroverts*.

iota—an infinitesimal amount, the smallest part, jot (Gk, ninth letter of the Greek alphabet)

*The champion showed not an **iota** of courtesy to the challenger during the weigh-in period, even though they had been friends and sparring partners.*

Iota is the smallest letter in the Greek alphabet.

J

jaundiced—yellowish (MF *jaune*, yellow, L *galbinus*, yellowish-green, from *galbus*, yellow)

***Jaundiced** people, who are affected by an abnormal flow of bile, usually have a yellowish cast to their skin.*

By extension, **jaundiced** can also mean having a hostile, envious or unfavorable view. Alexander Pope wrote that everything looks yellow to the **jaundiced** eye.

jocular—given to jesting, humorous, playful (L *jocularis*, from *joculus*, little jest, from *jocus*, joke)

*The comic's serious demeanor in his private life was belied by his **jocular** manner on stage.*

The word **jocund**, meaning merry, lively, pleasant, cheerful, has the same root.

joust—tournament, mock combat (OF *jouster*, to joust)

> *The roommates often engaged in good-natured verbal jousts.*

> Original **jousters** were knights on horseback who tried to knock their armored opponents to the ground.

judicious—wise, prudent (L *iudicium*, judgment)

> *A judicious choice of investments brought prosperity to Green in her later years.*
> *Judicious words and pacific actions finally brought an end to the community's conflict over a proposed housing development.*

juxtaposed—placed side by side (L *juxta*, near, next to, *positus*, placed)

> *When space is a consideration, office modules can be juxtaposed, but at the expense of privacy.*
> *In constructing neighborhoods, juxtaposing houses is more economical than building detached ones.*

K

kaleidoscope—infinite variety, a viewing instrument containing colored pieces of glass (Gk *kalos*, beautiful, *eidos*, form, *scopein*, view)

> *Betsy could amuse herself for a half-hour at a time with her favorite gift, a kaleidoscope.*

Sunset over the Grand Canyon was an unforgettable **kaleidoscope**.

keystone—wedge-shaped stone at the top of an arch

In baseball the **keystone** *sack is second base.*
Pennsylvania is nicknamed the **Keystone** *State because of its central geographic position among the original 13 colonies.*

kibbutz—a collective farm in Israel (Heb *gibbus*, gathering)

My friend Menachem lives on a **kibbutz** *near the Jordan River.*

The plural is **kibbutzim**.

On many **kibbutzim** *the adults' living quarters fan off a central dining hall and children's quarters.*

kinetic—relating to motion, active, lively (Gk *kinetos*, moving)

Elvis Presley had a **kinetic** *energy that communicated itself to the audience.*
Leonard Bernstein's **kinetic** *force was a predominant influence on 20th-century American music.*

kleptomania—irresistible urge to steal (Gk *kleptein*, steal)

Shoplifting may be **kleptomania**, *which is considered a sickness, but it is a crime nonetheless.*

kremlin—fortress or walled citadel of a Russian city (Russ *kreml*)

*Many cities had kremlins, but the **Kremlin** in Moscow is the most famous.*

The **Kremlin**, triangular and occupying 90 acres, was the residence of the czars until Peter the Great moved the capital of Russia to St. Petersburg (later Leningrad, but now St. Petersburg again). In 1918 the capital was transferred back to Moscow, and the **Kremlin** became the administrative and political focus of the Soviet Union.

kudos—renown, praise, fame (Gk *kydos*)

*Volunteer firefighters are quiet heroes who deserve much **kudos**.*

Merriam-Webster dictionaries say that **kudos** is both singular and plural. Although the plural verb is seldom used, this is a correct usage: "Throughout the year, Rachel received various other **kudos**, including her high school's prestigious scholar-athlete award for basketball." This 16-year-old dynamo also excels in softball and field hockey. She is also a proud member of the National Honor Society.

L

lacerate—to tear, rend, mangle (L *lacerere*, to tear)

*This latter-day Romeo claims that his heart bears many **lacerations**.*

---

*The skeletons of crabs and purple shells **lacerated** the honeymooning couple's bare feet as they walked on the Monterey beach.*

laconic—concise, undemonstrative, terse (Gk *Lakonikos*)

*As usual, the **laconic** George understated the seriousness of the situation.*

This word derives from Laconia, an ancient Greek district, of which Sparta was the capital. The Spartans were famous for their succinct way of speaking and writing. Philip, the King of Macedon, threatened them when he said "If I enter Laconia, I will raze it to the ground." The Spartan magistrates **laconically** replied, "If."

largo—slow, broad (It, from *largus*, generous, abundant)

*In music the **largo** movement is a particularly slow one.*

The cast of the 1948 movie thriller *Key **Largo*** included Humphrey Bogart, Lauren Bacall, Edward G. Robinson, Claire Trevor and Lionel Barrymore.

lassitude—weariness, lethargy, debility (I, *lassus*, weary)

*Sleeping sickness is characterized by **lassitude**.*

*Between cases, Sherlock Holmes suffered from a **lassitude** that made Dr. Watson, his companion, concerned that the detective might reawaken his addiction to cocaine.*

leonine—like a lion (L *leo*, lion)

> *The back of Leopold Stokowski's **leonine** head was immortalized in the film* Fantasia.
> *Some sphinxes had **leonine** heads. Others had the faces of women.*

lethargy—drowsiness, apathy (Gk *lethe*, forgetfulness)

> *Politicians complain that the American people seem to suffer from extreme **lethargy** on Election Day.*

This word comes from Greek mythology. Lethe was a place of oblivion in the lower world.

lexicographer—a maker of dictionaries, student of words (Gk *lexis*, word, *graphos*, writing)

> *Samuel Johnson and Noah Webster were two of the most prominent early **lexicographers**.*
> *Johnson called a **lexicographer** "a harmless drudge."*

A related word is **lexicon**, which you're looking at now.

liaison—close bond, interrelationship (F *lier*, to tie, bind, *aison*, ation)

> *Henry's group was the **liaison** between the airlines and the U.S. Department of Transportation.*

*Dangerous **Liaisons** is a magnificently crafted movie about depravity, cruelty and deceit among the aristocracy in pre-Revolutionary France.*

This film was adapted from a novel by Choderlos de Laclos titled *Les Liaisons Dangereuses*, which the author said was fully intended to shock. It succeeded then, and it still succeeds.

ligature—bond, connection (L *ligare*, to tie, bind)

> *Sutures are used as **ligatures** in surgery.*
> *In printing, **ligatures** are one or more letters of the alphabet joined or combined into one, for example, æ.*

Oliver Wendell Holmes, Sr., a physician who disliked pretentiousness, wrote that he would never use a long word where a short one would do. There were professors, he said, who **ligate** arteries. Other surgeons only tie them, and it stops the bleeding just as well.

lilliputian—tiny, small, undersized (from Lilliput, an imaginary country)

> *In his brilliant* Gulliver's Travels, *Jonathan Swift describes Gulliver's first journey, to **Lilliput**, where the **Lilliputians**, fearful of this giant, captured him and kept him in chains.*

Sometimes the adjective of **lilliputian** is spelled with a capital *L*.

logorrhea—excessive talkativeness, running off at the mouth (Gk *logos*, word, *rhea*, flowing)

> *Speakers should never succumb to the temptation of **logorrhea**.*

logotype—symbol used for identification (Gk *logos*, word, *typos*, impression, image, model, type)

> *A red flying horse is used as the **logotype** for Mobil gasoline.*

> This word is almost always abbreviated in speech to **logo**, meaning an individualized symbol for instant recognition. The *fleur-de-lis* is the **logo** of the Boy Scouts of America.

loquacious—talkative, garrulous (L *loquax*)

> *There is a time to keep silent and a time to speak, and even a time to be **loquacious**.*

lupine—wolfish, wolflike (L *lupus*, wolf)

> *Robin's friends thought that his sideburns gave him a **lupine** appearance.*
> *The stalker who haunted Chicago streets even had a **lupine** walk.*

M

magnanimous—generous in spirit (L *magnus*, great, *animus*, spirit)

> *Even enemies can be **magnanimous** in victory.*
> ***Magnanimity** is rarely foolish.*

malevolent—mean-spirited, injurious, filled with spite or hatred (L *male*, badly, *velle*, to will)

> *The clouds hovered over the ball park like* ***malevolent*** *spirits.*
>
> *Dorothy was frightened by the* ***malevolent*** *shrieks of the Wicked Witch, but she courageously refused to give up the ruby slippers.*

malign—to act maliciously, slander, vilify (L *male*)

> *Caldwell took the opportunity to* ***malign*** *his competitors, asserting that their goods were inferior.*
>
> *The vice president sued the newspaper, alleging that it had* ***maligned*** *him unfairly because of his stock trades.*

malleable—open-minded, impressionable, capable of being molded or transformed (L *malleare*, to hammer)

> *Youth should be* ***malleable***, *middle age should be confident and old age should be* ***malleable*** *once again.*

manumission—freeing, as of a slave (L *manu*, from the hand, *mittere*, to let go, send)

> *In the antebellum South,* ***manumission*** *for a price was practiced by the more greedy slaveowners.*
>
> *Tess celebrated her* ***manumission*** *from an oppressive relationship with Jack.*

masochism—extreme self-denial, self-punishment (from Leopold von Sacher-**Masoch**, a German novelist)

*Some critics consider ice hockey, with its attendant broken front teeth and frequent bloody melees, an exercise in **masochism**, while fans see it as a fast, exciting sport.*

masterful—domineering, arrogant, imperious (ME *maister*, master)

*General Scott's **masterful** command earned him the enmity of his subordinate officers.*
In the film The King and I, *Yul Brynner portrays the **masterful** King of Siam.*

This word is often mistakenly used to mean *masterly*. The two should be distinguished, since for most people—and society—it is more desirable to be *masterly* than **masterful**.

masterly—with the skill of a master, artistic, skillful, talented (ME *maister*, master)

*The museum exhibited the **masterly** works of Ansel Adams, whose black-and-white photographs made him preeminent in his field.*
*Michelangelo's **masterly** ceiling in the Sistine Chapel has never been equalled.*

mauseoleum—tomb, gloomy, ornate structure (Gk *mausoleion*)

*Napoleon's **mausoleum** is under the huge dome of the Hôtel des Invalides in Paris.*

*Probably the most famous of all **mausoleums** is the Taj Mahal at Agra, India.*

These structures are named after **Mausolos**, a Greek ruler in 353, whose tomb is in Halicarnassus.

The Invalides, a historic landmark in Paris, was originally a hospital for disabled veterans. It is now a military museum complex.

The Taj Mahal, ordered built by the Mogul emperor of India Shah Jahan, was completed in 1648 as a memorial to his beloved wife, Mumtaz Mahal. Deservedly considered one of the most beautiful buildings in the world, it is in a perfect state of preservation.

maven—connoisseur, expert, knowledgeable person (Y, from LHeb)

*An oenophile is a lover of wine or a wine **maven**.*
*Her best friend was a **maven** when it came to Italian cuisine.*
*Besides being a world-renowned playwright, George Bernard Shaw was a drama **maven**, and wrote many memorable reviews of other people's plays.*

maximal—highest, greatest, most effective (L *maximus*)

*To get the **maximal** effect from this medication, take it on an empty stomach.*
*The Marxists' motto was "The **maximal** good for the greatest number."*
*Some philosophers consider the Age of Enlightenment, characterized by human reason, to be the **maximal** period in European culture.*

mayhem—needless, malicious or willful damage or physical injury (ME *maym*, from Anglo-French *mahaim*)

> *The riots in Los Angeles were notorious for looting,* ***mayhem*** *and wanton cruelty.*
> *In the suit, the complainant said that the editorial had committed verbal* ***mayhem*** *on the candidate.*

megalith—huge prehistoric stone (Gk *megas*, great, strong, large, *lithos*, stone)

> *Each stone at Stonehenge, the eerie monument on Salisbury Plain in England, is a* ***megalith***.

melee—brawl, donnybrook, free-for-all (F *mélee*)

> *A bar dispute escalated into a* ***melee*** *on the busy street.*
> *Robin Hood's men merrily engaged in a* ***melee*** *with the Sheriff of Nottingham.*

mellifluous—honeyed, smooth, sweet (L *mel*, honey, *fluere*, to flow)

> *The* ***mellifluous*** *voices of Pavarotti, Domingo and Carreras blended in a magnificent trio from* Turandot.

The feminine name Melissa, as in Mercouri, the famous Greek movie star, is a descendant of the same root.

memento—keepsake, remembrance, souvenir (ME, from L, *memenisse*, to remember)

> ***Mementos*** *from the past are the heirlooms of the future.*

Tanya brought back a gold griffin pin from the Louvre as a **memento** *for her daughter.*

This word is often misspelled and mispronounced as "momentos."

memoir—report, record, personal narrative (F *mémoire,* from L *memoria,* memory)

Winston Churchill's **memoirs** *make fine reading. Many a movie star wishes another celebrity's* **memoir** *had gone unpublished.*

mentation—mental activity (L *mens,* mind)

Mentation *may be difficult after a heavy lunch.*

This word is a synonym for thinking or cerebration.

mercurial—temperamental, uneven, unpredictable, volatile (L *Mercurialis,* of the god or the planet of Mercury)

Certain ethnic groups or nationalities are falsely stereotyped as **mercurial**.

No doubt some members of these groups are **mercurial**, but the same could be said of any group.

Mercury, the ancient Roman god of commerce and the messenger of the gods, was noted for his eloquence, shrewdness, and ingenuity.

meretricious—false, pretentious, insincere (L *meretrix,* prostitute)

Politicians abound in **meretricious** *claims and promises.*

*The seemingly cordial relationship between top and middle management was in fact **meretricious**.*

mesmerize—hypnotize, spellbind, fascinate (from Franz Anton Mesmer; see commentary under *charlatan*)

*Even 40 years after Sputnik, the launch of a satellite into outer space is a **mesmerizing** sight.*
*The horseback ride of the nude Lady Godiva **mesmerized** one inhabitant of Coventry.*

This woman's husband promised to repeal his heavy taxes on the city of Coventry if she would ride naked through the city. Lady Godiva, famous in English history, rode through the streets with her nudity partially covered by her ankle-length golden hair. The inhabitants closed their shutters in sympathy with her. According to a later story, one person couldn't help peeking. He is immortalized by the nickname Peeping Tom.

metabolism—process of assimilation and nutrition in the body (G *metabolisch*, from Gk *metabolikos*, changing, from meta, with, after, ballein, throw)

*Nutritionists are concerned with the **metabolism** of certain substances such as iron, calcium and magnesium in the body.*

metaphor—figure of speech implying comparison, analogy or similarity (MF *metaphore*, from Gk *metapharein*, to transfer, change, from *meta*, with, after, *pharein*, to bear)

*Carl Sandburg's best-known **metaphor** is the Chicago fog coming in "on little cat feet."*

*Shakespeare used **metaphor** extensively and effectively in his sonnets: "Shall I compare thee to a summer's day?"*

metropolitan—relating to a city (LL, mother city, from Gk *metropolis*, from *metra* or *meter*, mother, *polis*, city)

*Washington, D.C., could be considered the **metropolis** of America.*

*Tokyo and Hong Kong have such a **metropolitan** feeling that the New Yorker felt right at home.*

As a noun, a **metropolitan** is the head of an ecclesiastic district of the Eastern Orthodox Church, especially one headquartered in a large city.

microcosm—miniature universe (ML *microcosmus*, from Gk *mikros kosmos*, small world)

*Aircraft carriers, ocean liners, and nuclear submarines are communities in themselves, **microcosms** of the larger world.*

*Television writers are enthralled by the **microcosmic** nature of medical centers, as can be seen by the spate of series about hospitals and emergency rooms.*

migraine—severe, excruciatingly painful headache (F, from LL *hemicrania*, pain in one side of the head, from Gk *hemi*, half, *kranion*, skull)

***Migraine**, although not life-threatening, is a scourge not confined to people with stressful occupations.*

Migraine cuts across all lines, not respecting age, sex, mental status or physical health. It is often accompanied by nausea and vomiting.

Some **migraineurs** know that a headache is coming on when they experience a familiar aura, with flashing lights before the eyes and other unpleasant symptoms.

milieu—environment, setting, midst (F, from L *medius*, middle, *locus*, place)

*Artists are sometimes troubled by the unfamiliar, cold **milieu** of the business world.*

*Competition was his **milieu**, and he thrived on it.*

millennium—a thousand years, period free of human imperfections (L *mille*, thousand, *annum*, year)

*Controversy swirls around whether the **millennium** starts in the year 2000 or the year 2001.*

Most people think 2000; purists and Stanley Kubrick fans, 2001.

If you have trouble remembering that this word has two *n*'s, think of *annual* and *biennial*.

minimal—the very least possible, extremely minute (L *minimus*, smallest)

*If tunnels were built by designers or workers with **minimal** skills or standards, they would never hold up under the tremendous weight they bear.*

misanthrope—one who hates or has contempt for humankind (Gk *misein*, to hate, *anthropos*, man, human being)

> *The rank hypocrisy Gale saw in his profession made him an undiscriminating misanthrope.*

> *A man may say he loves humankind, but if he hates his neighbor, he is a true misanthrope.*

misogynist—showing hatred or distrust of women (Gk *miso*, hatred, *gyne*, woman)

> *Many a misogynist has had an unhappy love affair.*

> *Andrew's misogyny dissipated as his friendship with Joan grew and he recognized her beauty of spirit.*

The counterpart of misogyny is *misandry* (Gk *mis*, hatred, *andros*, man), hatred or distrust of men.

mnemonic—helping to remember (Gk *mneme*, memory)

> *The mnemonic aid E G B D F, which stands for every good boy does fine, can be used by piano beginners to remember the lines in the G clef. F A C E is a mnemonic to remember the spaces.*

> *A checklist is a good mnemonic aid when completing each stage of an important project.*

Here's another **mnemonic** aid that may some day come in handy: Remember *story* for things historic and actual for things historical.

The origin of many words containing *mn*, including *amnesty* and *amnesia*, is **Mnemosyne**, the Greek goddess of memory.

modicum—a little bit, limited quantity (L *modicus*, moderate, small)

> A **modicum** *of good sense goes a long way in settling a dispute.*
> *Their tale of woe hasn't a* **modicum** *of truth.*

monogamy—one single marriage or mating (LL *monogamus*, marrying once)

> *Some societies in the world do not practice* **monogamy***. They sanction bigamy (usually two spouses) or polygamy (two or more spouses).*

monolith—a single huge stone or stone structure (Gk *mono*, single, alone, *lithos*, stone)

> *Two red granite obelisks from Egypt, nicknamed Cleopatra's Needles, were erected about 1475 BC in Heliopolis ("City of the Sun"). One is the* **monolith** *on the Thames River in London, and the other is in Central Park in New York City.*

> A related word is *aerolithology*, which is the science dealing with meteorites.

monosyllabic—having one syllable, terse, succinct (Gk *mono*, single, alone, *syllabe*, syllable)

> *One game that word experts play is to write* **monosyllabic** *essays, that is, works in which each word contains only one syllable. It's much harder than it sounds.*

---

*The Red Queen's order was pointedly **monosyllabic**: "Off with their heads!"*

moribund—dying, approaching death, dormant (L *moribundus*, from *mori*, to die

*Far from being **moribund**, the blacksmithing trade is still lively, especially the horseshoeing part of it.*

Ask any fan of horse racing.

morphology—the study of structure (Gk *morphe*, form, structure, *logos*, logy)

Morphology *includes many kinds of studies, among them the structure of words, cells, anatomy, plants and animals.*

mortify—humiliate, injure, destroy (L *mortificare*, from *mors*, death, *ficare*, to make, form into, make similar to, invest with the attributes of)

*The flesh can be **mortified** by disease, the spirit by constant humiliation.*
*In boot camp that day, the drill sergeant managed to **mortify** the entire squad with his brutal language*

mufti—civilian or street dress, especially when worn by those usually in military uniform (Ar)

*Ernest was glad to don **mufti** when he was on leave from Okinawa.*

mundane—worldly, relating to human concerns (L *mundus*, world)

> *Astronauts have to contend with such **mundane** things as eating and drinking even as they contend with weightlessness.*
> *The abbot urged the monks to abandon **mundane** thoughts and concentrate on spiritual matters.*

munificent—liberal, exceedingly generous (L *munificus*, generous, from *muni*, service, gift)

> *Many universities and medical centers bear the names of **munificent** donors.*

myopia—nearsightedness, lack of discernment (Gk)

> *Governments are often criticized for their **myopia** in foreign affairs.*
> ***Myopia** can be corrected by the proper eyeglasses.*

N

narcissism—egoism, excessive vanity (from **Narcissus**)

> ***Narcissus** was a handsome youth in Greco-Roman mythology who fell in love with his own reflection in the water, died of unrequited love, and was turned into the flower **narcissus**.*
> *The **narcissistic** impulses of adolescence are ordinarily outgrown in adulthood.*

nascent—being born, beginning to exist (L *nasci*, to be born)

> *In some Pacific islands, industrialization is in a* **nascent** *stage.*
>
> **Nascent** *stirrings of revolt were seen in the devastated cities.*

nauseous—causing nausea, sickening, disgusting (L *nausea*, seasickness, from Gk *naus*, ship)

> *The odor of sulfur resembles the smell of rotten eggs, and is* **nauseous** *in the extreme.*
>
> *Half the passengers,* **nauseated** *by the ceaseless rolling of the ship, remained in their cabins for the rest of the voyage.*

Things are **nauseous**, that is, *causing* nausea; *people* are **nauseated**, that is, *feeling* nausea. These words should be carefully differentiated. You wouldn't want to be considered **nauseous**.

negligent—careless, neglectful (L *negligere*, to neglect)

> *Because of the* **negligent** *handling of the dyes, the entire stock of silk had to be discarded.*
>
> *To forgive* **negligence** *is divine; to sue over it is much more common.*

neologism—new or recent coining, coined word or expression (F *né*, born, *logie*, logy, from L *natus*, born, Gk *neos*, new, recent, *logos*, word)

> *Smog is a* **neologism**, *combining* smoke *and* fog.

Chortle, a combination of *chuckle* and *snort*, is attributed to Lewis Carroll, the author of the witty and delightful children's stories *Alice's Adventures in Wonderland* and *Through the Looking Glass*.

Television has given us many **neologisms**. Some of the best known, including Trekkies (fans) and "beam me up," are from the *Star Trek* series.

Cyberspace, discussed in this book under the *c*'s, is a much used (and overused) **neologism**. Technologic advances bring many **neologisms**.

nepotism—favoritism toward one's family, especially in business or politics (F *népotisme*, from L *nepos*, grandson, nephew)

> *"I didn't get this job through **nepotism**," the would-be starlet insisted. "My father hired me."*
>
> *Although his grandfather was the president of the firm, Stewart never took advantage of **nepotism**. He learned the business from the ground up and eventually became a vice president.*
>
> *The citizens' commission sharply criticized the **nepotism** among members of the legislature, who had created lucrative jobs for their relatives.*

noisome—annoying, odorous, harmful, destructive, noxious (ME *noysome*, from *noy*, annoy)

> *Smoke from the chemical factory created a **noisome** environment for the nearby inhabitants.*

This word really has nothing to do with noise, except that excessive noise pollution can create a **noisome** neighborhood.

nostalgia—fondness for things past, homesickness (from Gk *nostos*, return home)

> *Nguyen confessed to a **nostalgia** for the cooking of her Vietnamese homeland.*

noxious—toxic, harmful, injurious (L *noxa*, damage, offense, from *nocere*, to harm)

> ***Noxious** influences were thought to be partially responsible for the boy's misdeeds.*

nuance—trace, subtle distinction, slight gradation (from MF, shade of color)

> *An expert dyer can distinguish the **nuances** in shades of red or blue.*
>
> *There is more than a **nuance** of difference between acting and emoting.*

numismatist—specialist in coins, coin collector (L *numisma*, money, coin)

> *In 1964, when the United States Mint stopped using silver in coins, many **numismatists** grumbled.*

Numismatists are often philatelists as well.

O

obnoxious—offensive, hateful, objectionable (L *ob*, to, toward, *noxius*, harmful)

> *Unkind comments are usually **obnoxious**.*

*Extremists' views are **obnoxious** to those who are moderate in their approach.*

obstreperous—loud, unruly, unmanageable, rowdy (L *ob*, to, against, *strepere*, to make noise)

*The party grew so **obstreperous** that the neighbors called police.*

Synonyms for **obstreperous** are *vociferous, turbulent* and *clamorous*.

obverse—the front of a coin, currency or medal (L *obvertere*, to turn toward)

*Quarters depict the head of George Washington on the **obverse**.*
***Obverse** you win, reverse you lose.*

octogenarian—person 80 to 89 years of age (L *octogenarius*, consisting of 80)

*Grandma (Anna Mary Robertson) Moses took up painting in her 70s, and continued her art even after she was no longer an **octogenarian**.*

People in their 90s are nonagenarians. On seeing a beautiful young woman passing by, the nonagenarian Oliver Wendell Holmes, Jr. exclaimed, "Oh, to be 70 again!"

octothorp—the symbol # (origin apocryphal; L *octo*, eight)

*The symbol #, the **octothorp**, is called the pound sign when used on the telephone dial.*

This handy, versatile symbol is also the number sign, a sharp in music, and the game tic-tac-toe.

oleaginous—oily (L *olea*, olive or olive tree)

*The **oleaginous** manner of the snake oil salesman offended the more sophisticated listeners, and even some of the naive.*

*The Valdez accident left an **oleaginous** slick that devastated most of the coastline.*

ombudsman—representative, advocate, proponent (Sw)

*Consumers can go to an **ombudsman** to hear their complaints and find remedies.*

*College students have access to an **ombudsman** or **ombudswoman** to redress grievances against the administration.*

omnivorous—eating everything (L *omni*, all, *vorare*, to devour)

***Omnivorous** readers are usually more successful in their careers and enjoyment of life than nonreaders.*

*Bernard Berenson was an **omnivorous** collector of art and antiques.*

onerous—oppressive, burdensome, heavy (L *onus*, burden)

*Air traffic controllers have **onerous** jobs.*

*"He's not **onerous**. He's my brother."*

onomatopoeia—forming words to imitate natural sounds (Gk *onoma*, name, *poila*, make)

> Meow, bowwow, tweet, roar, chirp, hiss, buzz *and* zoom *are* **onomatopoeic** *words.*
> *Homer was one of many poets fond of* **onomatopoeia***.*

opprobrium—dishonor, contempt, disgraceful or infamous act (L *ob*, to, toward, *probrum*, disgraceful act, reproach)

> *Vandals who scrawl graffiti are held up to public* **opprobrium***.*
> *Embezzlement is* **opprobrious***.*

opus—a work, usually of art, as in music (L)

> Messiah *was Handel's greatest* **opus***.*

> The Latin phrase for a great work is **magnum opus**. The plural of **opus** is either **opera** or **opuses**, but the latter word is rarely used.

oral—by mouth, spoken (L *os*, mouth)

> *Lawyers tell us that* **oral** *agreements or contracts are difficult to prove, and they therefore recommend written ones.*
> ***Oral*** *medicines are easier to take than injected ones.*

> This word can be confused with *aural*, which sounds exactly the same but relates to the ear, not the mouth.
> Verbal messages can be either **oral**, that is, spoken, or written. *Verbal* simply means *with words.* Communication can also be nonverbal (without words), for

instance, a wink of the eye, a shrug of the shoulders or an uplifted middle finger in traffic.

ordinal—having a specified number or rank in a series (L *ordo*, order)

First, third, fourth, tenth and twentieth are all **ordinal** *numbers.*

The corresponding cardinal numbers are one, three, four, ten, and twenty.

Ordinal numbers are also correctly written as 1st, 3rd, 4th, 20th, and so on, depending on house style.

ornithology—branch of zoology specializing in birds (Gk *ornith*, bird, *logos*, study)

Cornell University has one of the foremost centers of **ornithology** *in the United States.*

A knowledgeable forest ranger has a wide range of **ornithologic** *information.*

ostentatious—showy, flagrant, conspicuous (L *ostendere*, to show)

Diamond Jim Brady's **ostentation** *irritated his fellow financiers.*

James Buchanan Brady was famous for his collection of jewels, especially diamonds (many of which he wore), his enthusiastic participation in Broadway night life, and his enormous appetite. But he was also famous as a philanthropist. Among many other benefactions is a clinic at Johns Hopkins Hospital that bears his name.

ostracize—banish from society (Gk *ostrakon*, oyster, shell, earthen vessel, potsherd)

> *Hester Prynne, the protagonist in Hawthorne's* The Scarlet Letter, *was **ostracized** and forced to wear an "A" for adultery.*

> In ancient Greek times, citizens could vote once a year in the *agora* (marketplace) on whether to **ostracize** someone. Political or financial corruption was especially frowned upon. Potsherds were used as ballots. If 6,000 or more votes were cast and a majority voted for **ostracism**, that person was banished from the city temporarily.

otiose—futile, ineffective, idle (L *otium*, ease, leisure)

> *At one time the search for extraterrestrial intelligence was thought to be an **otiose** endeavor.*

overt—open, unconcealed, manifest (MF, from *ovrir*, to open)

> *The faces of the protesters showed **overt** hostility.*
> *The children's **overt** delight as they watched the white lion cubs tumbling was worth the long wait.*

> Covert is the opposite of **overt**.

oxymoron—contradiction, paradox, incongruity (Gk *oxymoros*, pointedly foolish, from *oxy*, sharp, keen, *moron*, dull, foolish)

> *The word **oxymoron** is itself an **oxymoron**.*

Examples of **oxymorons** are deafening silence, cruel kindness, jumbo shrimp, mini-supermarket, left-handed compliment, conspicuous absence, critical acclaim, favorite disease and guest host.

Cynics include as **oxymorons** the phrases military intelligence and business ethics.

P

paleography—study of old writings (Gk *palaios*, old, ancient, *graphia*, graphy)

Illuminated manuscripts are a favorite with **paleographers** *because of their extraordinary beauty.*

palestra—arena, gymnasium, stadium (Gk, from *palalein*, to wrestle)

Modern gymnasts, wrestlers and other athletes, like their counterparts in ancient Greece and Rome, perform in **palestras**.

The University of Pennsylvania basketball team plays in an old arena called the **Palestra**.

palimpsest—parchment or manuscript that has been erased and written over more than once (Gk *palin*, again, back, *psestos*, scraped, rubbed)

Previous writings can be discerned on some ancient **palimpsests**.

Be careful not to misspell this word "palimpset."

palindrome—word, phrase, number or sentence that reads the same backward and forward (Gk *palindromos*, running back again)

> *One of the most famous **palindromes** is the sentence "Able was I ere I saw Elba."*
>
> *Another **palindrome** is "A man, a plan, a canal—Panama."*

> Other examples of **palindromes** are the number 2468642, the names *Ada, Anna, Eve, Hannah* and *Lil*, and the words *boob, deed* and *level*.

palpable—touchable, easily discernible, evident (L *palpare*, stroke, caress)

> *The hostility between panelists was nearly **palpable**.*
>
> *An enlarged liver is **palpable** to the experienced physician.*

> The opposite of **palpable** is impalpable.

panacea—remedy, cure for all ills, a cure-all (Gk, *pan*, all, *akeisthai*, to heal)

> *A flat tax is no **panacea** for a nation's economic woes.*
>
> *Charlatans have the **panacea** for everything that ails their gullible customers.*
>
> *The nicotine patch is an aid, not a **panacea,** for people trying to quit smoking.*

pandemic—affecting many people over a wide region (Gk *pan*, all, *demos*, populace)

> *Malaria is **pandemic** in countries that are afflicted with hordes of mosquitoes.*

> An epidemic affects many members of a particular population simultaneously.

pandemonium—a riot, din, uproar, tumult (Gk *pan*, all, *daimon*, spirit, deity)

> *President Mandela's entrance into the auditorium created **pandemonium**.*

> This word comes from an epic poem by John Milton, *Paradise Lost*, in which he describes **Pandaemonium**, the capital of Hell.

paradigm—model, example, pattern (Gk *paradeiknynai*, to show side by side)

> *The genius Mozart is the **paradigm** of musicality.*
> *Medical professionals are expanding their **paradigm** of what constitutes health and healing.*

> John Simon, a brilliant critic of art and other endeavors, wrote a book titled ***Paradigms** Lost*, in which he reflects on the "decline of literacy."

paradox—person, sentiment, statement or principle that is self-contradictory (Gk *paradoxos*, contrary to expectation)

> *"Fighting for peace" is a **paradox**.*

*Jane Eyre was a **paradox**, her modest air belying her spirited actions.*

parameter—statistical or mathematical variable, a value or measure to be sought (Gk *para*, before, ahead, *metron*, measure)

*Many **parameters** must be determined before a population can be called civilized.*

This word should not be used to mean perimeter. See *perimeter*.

paramount—foremost, chief, supreme, preeminent (from OF *par*, through, *mont*, mountain)

*Pete Seeger was the **paramount** folk singer in the middle part of the 20th century.*
*The rescue of victims is always **paramount** in a firefighter's mind.*

paranormal—unusual, supernatural (Gk *para*, beyond, L *norma*, pattern, rule)

*Duke University has studied **paranormal** phenomena such as extrasensory perception (ESP) for many decades.*

parity—equality, equivalence (L *par*, equal)

*There should always be **parity** between power and responsibility.*
***Parity** in intelligence is impossible, but **parity** in opportunity is the goal.*

*To make for competitiveness and fan interest, sports leagues aim for **parity** among teams.*

parsimonious—frugal, excessively thrifty, stingy (L from *parcere*, to spare)

*Ebenezer Scrooge was well known for his **parsimonious**, mean-spirited ways.*

pathology—study of abnormality, especially diseases (Gk *pathos*, experience, emotion, suffering)

__Pathologists__ study the changes in tissues of human beings, both in life and in death.
*Forensic **pathology** is the study of changes in human tissue as they relate to criminal activities.*

Pathology also relates to emotional and mental illnesses.

patina—covering, coloring, film, usually green, on bronze or copper statues or other structures (L, shallow dish)

*Rodin's "The Thinker" is covered with a fine **patina** that enhances its appearance.*
*Her face bore the beautiful **patina** of age and character.*

patrician—noble, aristocratic, relating to gentle breeding (L *patres*, fathers)

*Until about 350 BC, only **patricians**, members of the original citizen families in ancient Rome, could become senators or consuls.*

*Laurence Olivier's **patrician** bearing was used to good advantage in such films as* Hamlet *and* Henry V.

paucity—scarcity, small number, smallness (L *paucus*, little)

*The **paucity** of rain eventually created deserts where once gardens bloomed.*

*Less affluent neighborhoods suffered from the **paucity** of retail establishments, mainly grocery stores.*

pedagogue—teacher, especially of children (Gk *paidagogos*, from *pais*, child, *agogos*, leader, escort, from *agein*, to lead)

*Morris Cogan, a **pedagogue** in the University of Pittsburgh Graduate School of Education, was an experienced teacher of teachers.*

***Pedagogy** is the art or discipline of educating.*

pediatrician—physician specializing in the treatment and care of children (Gk *pais*, child, *iatros*, physician)

*Dr. Benjamin Spock, born in 1903, is a renowned **pediatrician** whose "baby book" has sold in the millions.*

pejorative—derogatory, disparaging (L *pejorare*, to become worse)

*A left-handed compliment seems to be pleasing but is in reality **pejorative**.*

Jargon is not a **pejorative** word, since it merely means a specialized language for insiders. It can, however, be used **pejoratively**.

---

penchant—inclination, leaning (F *pencher*, to incline, bend, from L *pendere*, to weigh)

>*Children have a **penchant** for crayoning on walls.*
>*The amateur collector had a **penchant** for toy mechanical banks.*

penitent—atoning, expressing sorrow for offenses (L *paenitere*, to be sorry)

>*Laura's **penitent** face was all the apology her sister needed.*
>*Joe bought his brother a new Erector set as **penitence** for losing most of the pieces.*

pensive—thoughtful, reflective (F *penser*, to think, from L *pensare*, to weigh, consider, ponder)

>*Aisha was in a **pensive** mood as she sat in the bay window and looked out at the snow-covered hills.*

>The pansy (F *pensée*, thought) was given this name because it resembles a face.

penultimate—next to the last in a series (L *pene*, almost, *ultima*, last)

>*The **penultimate** book in the tetralogy was the most successful and widely read.*

>A common error is to see only the *ultimate* part of this polysyllabic word and overlook the fact that it means "*next to* the last." Another mistake is to think that **penultimate** means the best or the quintessential. It doesn't.

peregrination—wandering, journey, travel (L *peregrinari*, to travel in foreign lands, from *peregrinus*, pilgrim)

> *Queen Isabella's help made Marco Polo's* **peregrinations** *financially possible.*
> *Pilgrims to the Holy Land made their* **peregrination** *a fascinating journey into biblical history.*

perfunctory—routine, mechanical, apathetic, done as a duty (L *per* [completing], *fungi*, to perform)

> *The* **perfunctory** *manner of the officials at Ellis Island did little to dampen the happiness the Svensens felt on landing in the United States.*
> *Donna's interest in stamping envelopes was* **perfunctory**; *her real ambition was to be a candidate for city council.*

perimeter—circumference, boundary (F *périmetre*, from Gk *peri*, around, *metron*, measure)

> *Police were stationed on the* **perimeter** *of the playing field to discourage fans from rioting.*

> Be sure to distinguish this word from *parameter* (see entry on page 106).

peripatetic—itinerant, walking or moving from place to place (Gk *peri*, around, *patein*, walk)

> **Peripatetic** *preachers became scarce as the country's population grew and became more prosperous.*

Even today, some clergymen and physicians are **peripatetic**. A physician may serve as a locum tenens, that is, a substitute practitioner for an indefinite time. Should the occasion ever arise, you will know that the plural of the Latin phrase *locum tenens*, which means holding (tenens) the place (locum) of or substituting for, is locum tenentes.

The **peripatetic** "Johnny Appleseed" (John Chapman, 1774-1845), a pioneer who was born in Massachusetts, walked for 40 years through Ohio, Indiana and western Pennsylvania sowing apple seeds. There are many stories about this early environmentalist.

perquisite—privilege, profit (L *per*, thoroughly, *quaerere*, to seek, gain, obtain)

*One **perquisite** of middle management was the opportunity to buy company stock at a discount.*

*A company car is a **perquisite** of sales representatives in many firms.*

This word is often abbreviated as "perks." It should not be confused with *prerequisite*, which is something required at the outset.

perspicacious—having keen discernment (L *perspicere*, to see through)

*Anna Quindlen's **perspicacious** commentaries in* The New York Times *earned her a Pulitzer Prize in 1992.*

The noun is **perspicacity**.

phantasmagoria—constantly changing succession of real or imaginary things (F *phantasmagorie*, images that seem to be phantoms)

> *Thomas de Quincey's* Confessions of an English Opium Eater *originated in his own dreadful **phantasmagorias** as an addict.*

phenomenon—fact or event of scientific or cultural interest, extraordinary person (Gk *phanein*, to show)

> *A solar eclipse is a **phenomenon** that can damage the naked eye.*
>
> *Michael Jordan and Dennis Rodman are basketball **phenomena**; Wilt Chamberlain, Kareem Abdul-Jabbar (formerly Lew Alcindor) and Julius Erving (Dr. J) used to be.*

philately—stamp collection (Gk *philein*, to love, *ateleia*, tax exemption, immunity)

> ***Philately** is a benign obsession unless you bankrupt yourself pursuing it.*
>
> *Adam's childhood interest in **philately** brought him a huge profit later in life.*

In early times a postage stamp conferred *ateleia*, immunity from public duties, such as the mailing charge or tax.

philology—study of words (F *philologie*, from L *philologia*, love of talk, argument, from Gk *philologos*, love of words and learning)

> *Amateur **philologists** love word puzzles.*

Philology *is the study of literature, language as used in literature, and human speech.*

pigeonhole—to put into compartments (MF *pijon*, ME, *hole*)

Politicians are fond of **pigeonholing** *their constituents or thinking of them as blocs, but voters continue to cast their ballots as individuals.*

pixel—short for picture element

A **pixel** *is one of a group of small, distinct photographic elements that together make up an image.*
The number of **pixels** *on a monitor determines whether an image will be clear or diffuse.*

The shorthand **pix** (for *pictures*) was used in a memorable headline from *Variety*, the publication of show business: "Hix nix stix pix," which translates from showbiz language into "Country people don't like pictures about country people."

platitude—trite or stale remark (F *plat*, flat)

Commonplace people are fond of **platitudes**—*what others call small talk. "Hot enough for you?"*

Some **platitudes** are clichés.
Even the speech of the bumbler Polonius in *Hamlet* is full of wise, quotable sayings, which we rephrase and now unthinkingly characterize as **platitudes**: "Brevity is the soul of wit." "The apparel oft proclaims the man." "Neither a borrower nor a lender be." "This above all: to

thine own self be true, and it must follow, as the night the day, thou canst not then be false to any man."

pliable—bendable, capable of being molded or changed, flexible (MF *plier*, to bend)

> *Thornton's opinions were as **pliable** as wet clay.*
> *Twine is more **pliable** than vinyl-covered wire.*

> *Ply*, as in three-ply yarn, is from the same root as **pliable**.

poetaster—a failed or would-be poet, versifier (L *poeta*, poet, *aster*, one whose work is inferior)

> *These immature works indicate a **poetaster** rather than a real poet.*

> This word is sometimes mispronounced "poet-taster," but the emphasis should be on the *poet* part, with *aster*, denoting lack of art, pronounced like the flower.

pontificate—pronounce pompously, speak as an oracle (L *pontifex*, high priest, pope, literally bridgemaker, from *pons*, bridge, *facere*, to make, do)

> *Heads of state are expected to **pontificate**, and none can resist the temptation.*
> *Celebrities are often asked to **pontificate** on subjects about which they know little.*

> In ancient Rome the emperor was the **Pontifex** Maximus. After the ascendancy of Christianity, the

pope became the **Pontifex** Maximus or **Pontifex** Summus, the supreme or highest priest.

posthaste—with the greatest speed possible (*post*, courier)

> *When the Maple Leaf defenseman was slashed with a stick across his face, the coach sent **posthaste** for the team physician.*

potency—strength, power (L *potentia*)

> *Antibiotics are tested for **potency** as well as safety.*
> *Never underestimate the **potency** of words.*

potpourri—dried flowers, mixture, medley, unrelated matters (F *pot pourri*, from Sp *olla podrida*, rotten pot)

> *During the shipboard gala, the orchestra was asked to play a **potpourri** of Gershwin tunes.*
> *Barbara's book was a captivating **potpourri** of history, anecdote and fact.*

This word is correctly pronounced *poh-purr-ee*; *pot-purr-ee* is also correct but some consider it substandard.

pragmatic—practical, matter-of-fact (Gk *pragmatikos*, from *pragma*, deed, affair)

> *The **pragmatic** effects of false economy could be seen throughout the pine barrens.*
> *Known for his **pragmatic** bent, Thomas rarely philosophized but instead went about solving problems.*

The noun is **pragmatism**.

---

precipitate—hasty, premature (L from *praeceps*, headlong)

> *Gabriel tried not to be* **precipitate** *in his judgment of the facts.*

> Also see *precipitous*.

precipitous—very steep (L *precepitium*, precipice)

> *The* **precipitous** *descent from Machu Picchu left the climbers dusty and breathless.*
> *Ithaca, New York, has many* **precipitous** *gorges within the city limits.*

> An advertising executive, who is also a professor of communication at Ithaca College, coined the slogan "Ithaca is gorges."

prehensile—adapted for grasping or seizing (F *préhensile*, from L *prehendere*, to grasp, seize)

> *Monkeys seem to fly because their* **prehensile** *tails allow them to swing wide distances from tree to tree.*

prerequisite—something required beforehand (L *pre*, before, *requirere*, to need, seek for, inquire after)

> *One* **prerequisite** *for advanced composition is a working knowledge of style, usage, spelling, grammar and punctuation.*
> *A good memory is a* **prerequisite** *for actors.*

> **Prerequisites** is sometimes confused with *perquisites*, which is abbreviated "perks" and means privileges.

prestidigitator—magician, sleight-of-hand artist (F *preste*, nimble, quick, L *digitus*, finger)

> *Some clowns are also **prestidigitators**, and can find coins in people's ears.*

> Harry Houdini was the Great Prestidigitator, and some of his death-defying escape tricks have never been duplicated.

probity—honesty, uprightness, integrity (L *probus*, honest, virtuous)

> *Janet was known for her impeccable **probity** in dealing with colleagues.*
> ***Probity** is the prerequisite for special prosecutors, who have to avoid even the appearance of fault.*

prognosis—outlook, outcome, foreknowledge (Gk)

> *The **prognosis** for the nation's economy was good when the period of inflation ended.*
> *When the catcher's knee was injured in a collision at home plate, the long-term **prognosis** seemed bleak.*

prognosticate—to foretell, prophesy (ML *prognosticus*)

> *Weatherpeople do not **prognosticate**; they simply give you the odds on the weather.*
> *No one ever hears about the failures of oracles, astrologers and other prognosticators.*

> Because these **prognosticators** use generalities, some of what they say must be on the mark. The rest is left to the imagination of the audience.

Incidentally, weatherpeople are right 80 percent of the time—not bad.

prolix—talkative, wordy, repetitious (L *prolixus*, extended, protracted)

*Insurance policies, like many other legal documents, seem to be needlessly **prolix**.*

*Anton Bruckner's symphonies are magnificently **prolix**, with the motifs being repeated over and over.*

proprietary—owning privately (L *proprietas*, property)

***Proprietary** drugs are trademarked and are solely owned by the manufacturer.*

*Patent holders have **proprietary** ownership of their inventions for a specified time.*

propriety—decorum, appropriateness (MF *proprieté*, personal quality)

*Runnels questioned the **propriety** of searching someone's house without permission.*

*The Three Stooges were known for their slapstick, not their **propriety**.*

prowess—gallantry, bravery, excellence (ME *prouwesse*)

*Audie Murphy was the most decorated American soldier in World War II because of his **prowess** on the battlefield. He also appeared later in Hollywood films about the war.*

prudent—wise, farseeing, frugal (L *prudens*)

> ***Prudent*** *management mandates intelligent and compassionate treatment of its employees as well as its stockholders.*

> The noun is **prudence**.

pseudonym—pen name, fictitious name (Gk *pseudes*, false, *onyma*, name)

> *Elia was the **pseudonym** of the English essayist Charles Lamb.*
> *Mary Ann (or Marian) Evans took the **pseudonym** George Eliot.*
> *Gypsy Rose Lee, the most famous, and certainly most stylish, stripteaser, was the **pseudonym** of Rose Louise Hovick. Her sister, the actress June, changed her last name to the **pseudonym** Havoc when she came to Hollywood.*

> A synonym for **pseudonym** that is ordinarily reserved for writers is *nom de plume.*

pterodactyl—extinct flying reptile (Gk *pteron*, feather, wing, *daktylos*, finger, toe)

> *Dinosaur lovers like to build models of pterodactyls.*

punctilious—exact, careful in manners (Sp *puntillo*, small point)

> *In his usual **punctilious** manner, the host greeted each guest with courtly grace.*

pundit—learned person, teacher (Hindi *pandit*, from Skt *pandita*, learned, wise)

> *Blackwell is considered the **pundit** of bad taste because of his "Ten Worst-Dressed Actors" list.*

> Motilal Nehru, an Indian lawyer and political leader, was called **Pandit** Nehru. He became associated in 1919 with Mohandas (Mahatma, which means *great-souled*) Gandhi in the civil disobedience movement.

> Nehru's son, Jawaharlal Nehru, became Gandhi's political heir.

punitive—punishing (L *punire*, to punish)

> *The plaintiffs were awarded **punitive** damages in addition to compensatory damages because of the willful and malicious conduct of the defendant.*

> *Dissenters were subject to **punitive** measures that included jail time.*

putative—commonly accepted, reputed (L *putare*, to consider, think)

> Their **putative** marriage was in fact bigamous.

pyromaniac—arsonist, compulsive firestarter (Gk *pyr*, fire)

> *To the community's astonishment, a volunteer firefighter turned out to be a **pyromaniac**.*

Q

quadrilateral—four-sided, four-sided figure with four angles
(L *quattuor*, four, *latus*, side)

> *All rectangles are **quadrilateral**, but not all
> **quadrilaterals** are rectangles.*
>
> *The **quadrilateral** agreement fell apart when the
> two Eastern countries split with the two Western ones
> over fishing rights in international waters.*

quash—to suppress, crush, quell (L *cassus*, empty, void,
without effect)

> *The district judge denied the defense attorney's
> motion to **quash** the four-count indictment for
> embezzling.*
>
> *John Brown's antislavery rebellion was **quashed**
> when he and his 21 followers were captured at Harpers
> Ferry by U.S. marines led by Colonel Robert E. Lee.*

querulous—complaining, whining, irritable (L *querulus*,
complaining)

> *You can often divert **querulous** children with a
> shiny toy.*
>
> *Propaganda is sometimes more **querulous** than
> persuasive.*

quicksilver—mercurial, changeable, quick (ME *quik*, alive, silver, translated from L *argentum vivum*)

> *Roger's **quicksilver** moods were like the northeastern weather—one moment sunny, the next gloomy.*

> *The chameleon's movements were like **quicksilver**.*

quintessence—distillation, epitome, the most typical example, purest of its kind (L *quinta*, fifth, *essentia*, essence)

> *Judge Learned Hand's opinions from the United States Court of Appeals were the **quintessence** of reason and compassion.*

> The adjective is **quintessential**.

> *Fred Astaire was the **quintessential** dancer.*

R

ramifications—consequences, subdivisions, developments (L *ramus*, branch, *ificare*, -ify, to make, perform)

> *The **ramifications** of late-night carousing can be disastrous.*

> *Family trees are so **ramified** that it takes an expert or a dedicated amateur to unravel the relationships.*

> *The blood vessels of the heart have innumerable **ramifications**.*

recidivism—relapse into previous behavior (L *recidivus*, falling back, recurring)

> *Unemployment and moral poverty are direct causes of recidivism among criminals.*
> *Recidivist tendencies can be seen in Elizabeth Taylor, Mickey Rooney and others who engage in multiple marriages.*

reciprocal—mutually shared (L *reciprocus*, returning the same way)

> *Some states have reciprocal agreements on legal or medical certification and on traffic tickets.*
> *Reciprocity is the life of trade.*

regime—reigning period, era, social or political system (F *régime*, from L *regimen*)

> *During his 43-year regime, Peter the Great established shipbuilding as a prime industry for Russia, encouraged Western influences, and was instrumental in transforming medieval Muscovy into modern Russia.*
> *Boss Tweed's regime was characterized by greed, corruption, bribery and graft.*

regimen—systematic plan, regulation or treatment (L *regere*, to rule)

> *The antisepsis regimen established in the last decades of the 19th century by Semmelweis—requiring frequent washing of hands, especially during childbirth—drastically reduced the mumber of maternal deaths from infectious disease.*

---

remuneration—payment, reward, gift, recompense (L *munus*, gift)

> *The **remuneration** for a good conscience is, alas, nothing more than a good night's sleep.*
> *Henri's business became more **remunerative** when he acquired the best stylist on Fifth Avenue.*

renascence—rebirth (L *renasci*, to be born again)

> *In middle age the couple had a **renascence** of interest in musical comedy.*

The *Renaissance*, which means exactly the same as **renascence**, usually refers to the transitional period in Europe between the 14th and 17th centuries, which saw the flourishing of literature and the arts and the beginnings of modern science.

repartee—clever retort, witty reply (F *repartie*)

> *Johnny Carson was noted for his **repartee** with* Tonight Show *guests.*

Dorothy Parker, a member of the Algonquin (Hotel) Round Table, was a drama critic as famous for her **repartee** as for her acerbic reviews. Perhaps the best-known review was the one in which she wrote that the actress "ran the whole gamut of emotions from A to B."

reticent—quiet, silent, reserved in speech (L *reticere*, to keep silent)

> *Modesty often goes with **reticence**.*

*Abe Lincoln was by nature **reticent**, but he could outgoing and jovial when the occasion stirred him.*

retroactive—going back before a specified time (L *retro*, back, *agere*, to drive, act)

*The reinstated workers were entitled to **retroactive** pay to compensate them for time lost when the factory burned down.*

*Because there was no statute of limitations, the business privilege tax could be levied **retroactively**.*

rhinitis—inflammation of the nasal mucous membranes (Gk *rhis*, nose, *itis*, inflammation)

*Seasonal **rhinitis** refers to allergic reactions brought on by pollen and other airborne pollutants.*

The word *rhinoceros* comes from the Greek *rhino*, nose, and *keras*, horn. This well-named, ponderous animal has a horn on its nose.

risible—funny, laughable, laughter-provoking, ridiculous (L *risus*, from *ridere*, to laugh)

*The television comedy series Murphy Brown always tickled his **risible** sense.*

*Life would be dull if it were not for our **risibilities**.*

robot—machine that can duplicate some human activities (Czech *robota*, forced work, labor)

*Today many industries use **robots** or **robotic** machinery to do repetitive, heavy work.*

*Police bomb details use **robots** to retrieve bombs or suspected explosives and to defuse them or blow them up.*

A forerunner of Isaac Asimov's *I, **Robot*** was a famous drama, *R.U.R.,* by the Czechoslovakian humanist and playwright Karel Capek.

R.U.R. stood for Rossum's Universal Robots. Capek's play (1921, translated into English in 1923) introduced the word **robot** into our language.

rote—memorizing (ME *rote,* custom)

The entire class had to recite all 52 verses of The Bells of Atri, *an epic poem, by **rote**.*

*Patriotism cannot be taught—or learned—by **rote**.*

rufous—red, reddish (L *rufus*)

*The **rufous** plumage and flight of the cardinals delighted the city-dwellers every morning.*

*Thomas Jefferson's **rufous** hair made him conspicuous among the older signers of the Declaration.*

ruthless—merciless, without pity or compassion (ME *rewthe,* pity, *les,* less, without)

*The **ruthless** onslaught of words was too much for Don's fragile ego.*

*Rare timberland in the Northwest became the target of **ruthless** deforestation.*

S

sadism—gratification from cruelty, excessive mental or physical cruelty (from the Comte [Marquis] de Sade, French author)

> *Sadism is the last refuge of the coward.*
> *The phenomenon of sadism has been studied as a precursor to the teachings of Freud and Nietzsche.*

salutary—wholesome, healthful, curative (L *salus*, health, safety)

> *American Indians were well aware of the salutary effects of certain herbs on disease and injuries.*
> *Improved nutrition is a salutary factor in the education of small children.*

salutatory—welcoming speech (L *salutare*, to salute)

> *To Jonathan's surprise and pleasure, he was chosen to give the salutatory at commencement exercises.*

sanctimonious—hypocritically or falsely pious (L *sanctimonia*, sanctimony, from *sanctus*, holy)

> *Rasputin was a sanctimonious charlatan, a monk without a conscience.*
> *Elmer Gantry's sanctimonious mouthings won him a gullible audience.*

sanction—to ratify, approve, confirm (MF, from L *sancire*, to decree, make sacred)

> *King John, forced by the barons to **sanction** the Magna Carta, signed it at Runnymede.*

The verb to **sanction** is to approve. Oddly enough, the plural noun **sanctions** means the opposite: coercive measures to punish nations that violate international law, such as trade **sanctions**, which impose an embargo or boycott against a rogue nation.

sanctum—a study, holy or sacred place, refuge, place of retreat or respite (L *sanctus*, holy)

> *The city editor closed the door of his **sanctum** to discourage unwelcome visitors.*
>
> *Antonia's studio was her **sanctum** sanctorum, her holy of holies, not to be trespassed upon except in a dire emergency.*

sanguinary—bloody, gory, murderous (L *sanguis*, blood)

> *For Americans, the Civil War was the most **sanguinary** conflict of any in United States history, including World War II.*

sanguine—optimistic, confident, cheerful (L *sanguis*, blood)

> *Wilkins Micawber, a character in Dickens's* David Copperfield, *had a **sanguine** outlook despite his poor financial circumstances. He was eternally certain that "something will turn up."*

satiate—to fill up, satisfy, overfill (L *satis*, enough)

> *Holiday candy can **satiate** the greatest chocolate-lover.*

> The noun is **satiety**.

schism—division, gap, separation, discord (Gk *schizein*, to split)

> *When Gordon became head of the national committee, the **schism** over states' rights widened, and the party eventually splintered into two factions.*
> *The **schism** between liberals and conservatives made bitter enemies of former friends.*

> **Schism** is pronounced *siz-im*, as in *scissors*, with the accent on the first syllable.

scintillate—to sparkle (L *scintillare*, to emit sparks)

> *City lights obscure the **scintillating** stars, but they're there just the same.*
> *The **scintillating** wit and humor of the pianist Victor Borge have earned him the nickname the Clown Prince of Denmark.*

> In one of his famous monologues, the Great Dane told his audience, "It's a sobering thought that when Mozart was my age, he had been dead 10 years."

scion—descendant, child, shoot of a plant (OHG *chinan*, to sprout)

> *Justice Oliver Wendell Holmes, himself a brilliant writer, was the worthy **scion** of his namesake, who was both a renowned physician and a man of letters.*

scurrilous—vulgar, evil, slanderous (L *scurrilus*, jeering)

> *Too many talk-show hosts are notorious for using* **scurrilous** *innuendo in their broadcasts.*

segue—(SEG-way) to go from one theme or song to another without pausing (It *seguire*, to follow, from L *sequi*)

> *Talented singers can* **segue** *from classical to popular music with no trouble at all.*
> *The director* **segued** *from the scene in the forest to the love scene in the house.*

semiannual—every six months or twice a year (L *semi*, half, *annum*, year)

> *Shoppers flocked to center-city for the* **semiannual** *sales in the department stores.*
> *Don't forget to go to the doctor for your* **semiannual** *checkup.*

> *Biannual* also means twice a year, but is seldom used, because it might be confused with *biennial*, which means every two years or every other year.

sempiternal—everlasting, eternal, never-ending (L *sempiternus*, eternal, from *semper*, always)

> *The* **sempiternal** *redwood trees in California, often towering more than 300 feet, are an awesome sight.*

septuagenarian—person between 70 and 79 years of age (L *septuaginta*, seventy, from *septem*, seven)

> *Many* **septuagenarians** *frown on retirement, and they continue to work at their occupations indefinitely.*

George Walker, a **septuagenarian**, is the first African American to win a Pulitzer Prize in music. His work *Lilacs* is based on Walt Whitman's *When Lilacs Last in the Dooryard Bloom'd*, an elegy for Lincoln. Walker was also the first African American graduate of the Curtis Institute of Music in Philadelphia.

serendipity—a fortunate or valuable finding by chance

One of the greatest instances of **serendipity** *in all history was the discovery of America by Christopher Columbus, who was looking for the Indies.*

Ceylon (now Sri Lanka) was formerly called **Serendip**. The word **serendipity**, coined by Horace Walpole, stems from a Persian fairy tale about three princes of Serendip who made random discoveries in their travels.

Serendipity played an important role in the discovery of Teflon on April 6, 1938 by Roy Plunkett, a young chemist working for the duPont company, who had received his Ph.D. degree just two years before.

Plunkett and his colleague, Jack Rebok, were experimenting to find a nontoxic refrigerant when they came across an empty tank that wasn't supposed to be empty. On examining the tank, they discovered a waxy white powder that had unexpectedly polymerized and had become polytetrafluoroethylene (Teflon), the material that "nothing will stick to."

The new material was originally used during World War II for gaskets in atom bombs. Today Teflon (*always* use a capital T, or you may get a letter from duPont) is used for everything from frying pans to heart valves and other artificial body parts. It is one of the few prosthetic substances that humans do not ordinarily reject.

Ronald Reagan is often dubbed the "Teflon president."

sesquicentennial—a 150th anniversary (L *sesqui*, one and a half, *centum*, hundred)

> *St. Augustine, Florida, the oldest city in the United States, celebrated the **sesquicentennial** of its incorporation in 1974, but it was founded long before that, in 1565.*

sesquipedalian—a very long word (L *sesquipedalis*, a foot and a half long, from *sesqui*, one and a half, *pes*, foot)

> *William F. Buckley is fond of **sesquipedalian** words, and uses them constantly in his columns, books and television appearances.*

shalom—hello, goodbye, welcome (Heb, well-being, peace)

> *In Israel and elsewhere in the world, **shalom** is like* aloha *in Hawaii—it serves as welcome, farewell and a wish that peace be with you.*

sibling—brother or sister (OE *sibb*, kinship)

> ***Sibling** rivalry is often used as an excuse for lack of civility.*

silicon—nonmetallic element in the earth's crust (from L *silex*, hard stone, flint, *on*, as in *carbon*)

> *Linus Pauling wrote that **silicon** plays an important role in the inorganic world, similar to that of carbon in the organic world.*

Silicon is used extensively for parts in computers and other machines. **Silicon** Valley is so called because computer companies are clustered there.

sinecure—easy job, position (ML *sine cura*, without cure [of souls])

> *The idle repairman pictured in the Maytag television commercials has a **sinecure**.*
>
> *Being CEO of a worldwide company, Bill Gates said, is no **sinecure**.*

sinister—on the left side, left, evil, unlucky, inauspicious (L)

> *As Jessica entered the darkened room, she sensed a **sinister** presence near the window.*

In unenlightened times, left-handedness and some things on the left were thought to be abnormal or unlucky. The Latin word *dexter*, meaning right or on the right side, is the antonym or opposite of **sinister**. *Dextrous* (also correctly spelled *dexterous*) means not only right-handed or right-sided but skillful or clever as well.

Sistine—(NL *sixtinus*, from *sextus*, sixth)

The word **Sistine** refers to any of the several popes named Sixtus. The **Sistine** Chapel in the Vatican was built in 1473 for Pope Sixtus IV.

sodality—club, comradeship, association (L *sodalis*, comrade)

> *Many **sodalities** are formed for charitable purposes.*

solace—comfort, especially in grief or misfortune (L *solari*, to console, comfort)

> *After the death of his 6-year-old daughter, George found solace in working harder than ever.*

solecism—error or absurdity in usage or words, impropriety (Gk *soloikos*, speaking incorrectly)

> *Professor Henry Higgins set about correcting Liza Doolittle's solecisms and transforming her into an elegant lady.*

The Greek word *soloikos* originated with the citizens of Soloi, a city in ancient Greece, who were notorious for speaking their language incorrectly. A whole city of Mrs. Malaprops?

soliloquy—monologue, talking to oneself (L *soli*, alone, *loqui*, to speak)

> *Hamlet's soliloquy is so familiar and well known that many people can recite parts of it by heart.*

When her friend caught her talking to herself, Gina retorted, "Well, I like an intelligent audience."

solipsism—obsessive or extreme self-centeredness (L *solus*, alone, *ipse*, self)

> *It was evident from her solipsism that she felt the universe revolved around her.*

The adjective is **solipsistic**.

solon—lawgiver, legislator (Gk)

> *The Athenian lawgiver **Solon** was called one of the Seven Wise Men of Greece.*
> *Apathetic citizens are often ill served by the **solons** they keep returning to office.*

soporific—sleep-producing, boring (L *sopor*, deep sleep, *ificare*, producing, making)

> *Stale air can be **soporific** for captive listeners.*
> ***Soporific** medications should be taken about an hour before you go to bed.*

sorority—sisterhood (L *soror*, sister)

> ***Sorority** and fraternity chapters are identified by combinations of Greek letters.*

sparse—scarce, thin, scanty (L *sparsus*)

> *Vegetation is usually **sparse** in regions that have little rainfall.*
> *The northwestern mountainous states are **sparsely** populated.*

spatial—relating to space (L *spatium*, space)

> ***Spatial** perception is important for driving skill.*

spurious—false, bogus, fake, counterfeit (LL *spurius*, false)

> *Claims to the gold fields were sometimes **spurious**, but were maintained at gunpoint.*

---

*In contradistinction to the old Ben Franklins, with their fancy curlicues, the new $100 bills have so much bare space that they look **spurious**.*

stannous—containing or relating to tin (LL *stannum*, tin)

*Pewter is a **stannous** alloy, hardened with antimony and copper, and is used extensively for artware.*

stigma—stain, disgrace, identifying mark (L *stigma*, mark, brand)

*Cain forever bore the **stigma** of his brother Abel's murder.*

The usual plural is **stigmata**, but **stigmas** is also correct.

stygian—gloomy, hellish, infernal (L *stygius*, Gk *stygios*)

*Hansel and Gretel lost their way in the **stygian** darkness of the woods.*

The adjective **stygian** is taken from the Styx, a mythologic river in the subterranean world of the dead.

subliminal—outside ordinary perception, influencing behavior in subconscious ways (L *sub*, under, *limen*, threshold)

*Manufacturers use **subliminal** advertising in persuading consumers to buy their products.*
*The Judas kiss of Terry's sister-in-law sent her an ominous **subliminal** message.*

sublingual—under the tongue (L *sub*, under, *lingua*, tongue)

> *Certain drugs are made to be taken **sublingually** and to melt in the mouth.*

subtle—delicate, elusive, skillful, ingenious (L *subtilis*, finely woven, fine, refined, keen)

> *Manet was skillful in capturing the **subtle** color changes in the landscape at different times of day.*
>
> *Diplomacy calls for **subtlety** rather than confrontation.*
>
> *The courtroom image of a prisoner in leg irons and looking disheveled sends a **subtle**, although sometimes incorrect, message to the jury pool.*

succinct—terse, brief, concise (L *succingere*, to bind up)

> *For best effect, most proverbs are **succinct**.*

supercilious—condescending, haughty (L *super*, above, *cilia*, eyebrows)

> *A **supercilious** manner is not conducive to friendly relations.*

supersede—replace, supplant, take the place of (L *super*, above, *sedere* to sit)

> *The railroad and the telegraph **superseded** the short-lived Pony Express, which was gradually discontinued about 1861.*

Note that **supersede** is the only word in the English language with that root that ends in -*sede*. Only three words with that root end in -*ceed*: *exceed*, *proceed* and *succeed*. All other words in the language with that root end in -*cede*, for example, *secede*, *accede* and *intercede*.

surreptitious—secret, stealthy (L *sub*, secretly, under, *rapere*, to seize)

> *Foreign countries that engage in* **surreptitious** *or open pirating of videocassettes may be subject to severe sanctions.*

sybarite—a person who considers pleasure the most important thing in life (from Sybaris, an ancient Greek city in southern Italy)

> *One day at the spa hardly qualifies Jennifer as a* **sybarite**.

The citizens of Sybaris were famous for their love of luxury and pleasure.

Sybarites and hedonists have a common philosophy.

sycophant—scoundrel, talebearer, parasite, yea-sayer, bootlicker (Gk *sykon*, fig, *phainein*, to reveal, show)

> *The pejorative term* **sycophant** *is often applied to yes-men, who laugh at their bosses' jokes and tell tales on their co-workers.*

The fig part of this word's etymology comes from the Greek custom of gesturing with a fig to indicate a scoundrel.

symbiosis—cooperation, living together of two dissimilar entities or organisms (Gk *syn*, together with, with, *bios*, life)

> *The **symbiosis** of volunteerism and philanthropy is beneficial to any community.*
>
> *Remoras and sharks typify underwater **symbiosis**.*

syndrome—concurrence, a group of symptoms or signs, usually relating to diseases or disorders (Gk *syn*, together, with, *dramein*, to run)

> *The Huck Finn **syndrome** includes a child's truancy and a neglect of duties or obligations.*

After decades of working at a difficult or frustrating profession, some people experience the symptoms of burnout **syndrome**, including loss of interest and efficiency, extreme fatigue, impaired appetite and insomnia.

synergy—working together (Gk *syn*, together, with, *ergon*, work)

> *During World War II, government, industry, and labor showed extraordinary **synergy** in turning out products necessary for waging a multicontinental war.*
>
> *Caffeine is a **synergistic** drug that works in harmony with painkillers to relieve severe headache.*

The shoulder and back muscles work **synergistically** in weight-lifting.

T

taciturn—reticent, silent, laconic (F *taciturne*, from L *tacere*, to be silent)

> *A **taciturn** person is more likely to keep secrets than a talkative one.*
> *A **taciturn** master of ceremonies is an oxymoron.*

tantamount—equivalent, amounting to as much (AF *tant amounter*, to amount to as much)

> *Being nominated for office in that Democratic county is **tantamount** to being elected by acclamation.*

tautology—redundancy, repetition (Gk *tautos*, the same, from *to auto*, the same)

> ***Tautology** is hearing the lecturer say, "Before I speak, I'd like to say a few words."*

> Examples of **tautology** are phrases such as "red in color," "oval-shaped," handsome-looking," "basic fundamentals" and "the ultimate in perfection."

temporal—relating to time, fleeting, temporary, earthly (L *tempus*, time, period of time)

> *A clergyman's duty is to deal with spiritual matters, but these often turn out to be intertwined with **temporal** concerns.*
> *The **temporal** life of newspapers is short.*

tendentious—biased, tending or attempting to persuade
(from ML *tendentia*, tendency)

> *Propaganda is by definition **tendentious**.*
>
> *Being **tendentious** is an asset for insurance salesmen.*

tendinitis—inflammation of a tendon (L *tendo*, tendon)

> *After years of play, many baseball pitchers and tennis players suffer from **tendinitis** in the elbow.*
>
> ***Tendinitis** in the hands can mean the end of a musician's career.*

Tendonitis is also correct, but the spelling is seldom seen in medical contexts.

tetralogy—group of four connected works or four symptoms in a disorder or disease (Gk *tetra*, four, *logia*, logy)

> *Gloria's autobiography was a **tetralogy**, describing in intimate detail her childhood and adolescence in Illinois, her rise in New York as a dramatic actress, her brilliant career as a star in Hollywood, and her graceful retirement from the screen at age 64 to her home in Connecticut.*
>
> *The **tetralogy** of Fallot, named for the French physician who first described it, includes four main abnormalities of the heart.*
>
> *Botticelli's **tetralogy**, mythologic paintings of exquisite beauty, consists of* Spring (Primavera), The Birth of Venus, Mars and Venus, *and* Pallas Subduing a Centaur.

thespian—actor (from *Thespis*)

> *Drama schools and repertory theaters for aspiring* ***thespians*** *abound in the United States.*

> Thespis was a 6th-century BC Greek poet, who may have originated the actor's role in the theater.

titillate—to please, stimulate, tickle (L *tittilare*, to tickle)

> *Ice-dancing is certain to* ***titillate*** *the spectator with its beauty and grace as well as its athleticism.*
> *True comedy* ***titillates*** *only those with a well-developed sense of humor.*

titular—nominal, in name only, title (from L *titulus*, title)

> *With the election of a hostile legislature, Cheswick became only the* ***titular*** *head of the party.*
> *Steve Martin had the* ***titular*** *role in the movie remake of* Sergeant Bilko.

tortuous—winding, twisted, crooked, devious, circuitous (L *tortuosus*, tortuous, from *torquere*, to twist)

> *Lombard Street is the most* ***tortuous*** *street in San Francisco and perhaps in the United States, but a Cadillac can negotiate the downhill run—carefully, very carefully.*
> *Even philosophy majors can have difficulty following Kant's* ***tortuous*** *reasoning.*

Although **tortuous** and *torturous* are from the same Latin root, keep the two words distinct. *Torturous* means causing torture or extreme pain.

toxic—poisonous, harmful, polluting (L *toxicum*, poison)

> *Tobacco smoke contains carbon monoxide, nicotine, cyanide, nitric oxide, and many more* **toxic** *or carcinogenic substances.*
>
> *Psychotherapists see many clients scarred by their upbringing in* **toxic** *families.*

transcend—to go beyond, exceed, surpass (L *transcendere*, to climb across, surmount, from *trans*, across, beyond, *scandere*, to climb)

> *Civility* **transcends** *good manners.*
>
> *Superb acting* **transcends** *physical likeness and the accurate recitation of lines.*

translucent—transparent, partly transparent, shining through (L *trans*, through, *lucere*, to shine)

> *The turquoise waters of the Caribbean Sea are so* **translucent** *that you can see the fish swimming below. In your explanations, strive for* **translucency**.

transvestite—a cross-dresser, one who is addicted to the garb of the opposite sex (L *trans*, across, *vestire*, to clothe)

> **Transvestites** *are in great demand in the theater as female impersonators.*

trauma—a wound, injury, harm, damage (Gk wound)

> *The* **trauma** *of the Civil War never healed for the Prentiss family, which had lost three sons.*

*Psychologic **traumata** are nearly impossible to eradicate without proper treatment.*

Traumas is also a correct plural.

Trekkie—a fan of the science fiction television series *Star Trek*

*Each year **Trekkies** hold a national convention, at which they enjoy buying memorabilia, meeting Bill Shatner, and even dressing like the* Star Trek *characters.*

triage—selecting, sifting, choosing (F, from *trier*, to sift, pick out)

*Workers in the emergency department acted as a **triage** unit when the accident victims started to flood in, first treating those whose airways were obstructed and then the bleeding patients.*

This word is pronounced *tree-ahjh*, with a slight accent on the second syllable.

triceratops—an herbivorous dinosaur with three horns (L *tri*, three, Gk *keras*, horn, *ops*, eye, face)

*Daniel's favorite dinosaur models were the **triceratops** and the tyrannosaur (*Tyrannosaurus rex, Gk tyrannos, *tyrant*, rex, *king*)*.

trilogy—group of three related things or works (Gk *tri*, three, *logia*, logy)

*Isaac Asimov's landmark science fiction **trilogy**,* The Foundation, *was followed by a fourth work,* Foundation's Edge, *making the body of work a tetralogy.*

trimester—period of three months or thereabouts (L *tri*, three, *mensis*, month)

> *Examinations for certification were traditionally held at the beginning of the third scholastic **trimester**.*
>
> *Most states ban abortions during the third **trimester** of pregnancy.*

triskaidekaphobia—abnormal fear of the number 13 (Gk *triskaideka*, thirteen, *phobia*, fear)

> *Some builders are **triskaidekaphobic**, and therefore omit the 13th floor of buildings, going from the 12th to the 14th in one easy, or uneasy, leap.*

triumvirate—group or association of three persons (from L *trium*, of three, *vir*, man)

> *The best-known **triumvirate** in classical music consists of Bach, Beethoven and Brahms.*
>
> *Violations of constitutional law were heard by a **triumvirate** of learned jurists.*

> The word *tribunal* means a group of three persons hearing a case or matter.

truncate—shorten, condense (L *truncare*, to cut off, mutilate)

> *An evening of dancing was **truncated** by the abrupt departure of the band in a huff, 1996 model.*
>
> *In printouts, computer programs often **truncate** long names.*

U

ubiquitous—widespread, universal, being everywhere at the same time (L *ubique*, everywhere)

> *Jean Valjean, the hero of Victor Hugo's* Les Miserables, *was hounded for decades by the seemingly* **ubiquitous** *detective Javert.*
>
> *The township contemplated legislation banning the* **ubiquitous** *highway billboards.*

ultimatum—a final demand or condition (L *ultimas*, last, final)

> *Rejecting the* **ultimatum**, *the generals foolishly decided that war was the only alternative.*

ultrasound—waves with sound beyond the range of human hearing (L *ultra*, beyond, *sonus*, sound)

> **Ultrasound** *procedures are used extensively in medical practice.*

umbrage—resentment, displeasure (L *umbra*, shade, shadow)

> *Jackie Gleason said you should never take* **umbrage** *unless you can lick the guy.*

unilateral—one-sided (L *uni*, one, *latus*, side)

> *The lion makes a* **unilateral** *decision in dividing the prey.*

Couples in which one spouse or the other makes **unilateral** *decisions often wind up in the marriage counselor's office.*

ursine—bearlike (L *ursus*, bear)

Marty shambled in with his strange, **ursine** *walk and went immediately to his place at the dinner table.*

V

vacillate—waver, hesitate (L *vacillare*, to sway, waver)

Never **vacillate** *in your search for the truth.*

The noun is **vacillation**.

vagary—unpredictable, eccentric or capricious action (L *vagus*, wandering)

Dancing about in the moonlight was only one of the **vagaries** *of the Sansouci family.*

Vagaries usually come in bunches. Hardly anyone has just a single **vagary**.

valedictory—farewell speech (L *vale*, farewell, *dicere*, to say)

President Eisenhower, in his **valedictory**, *warned of the military-industrial complex.*

In his ***valedictory*** *speech, usually called his Farewell Address, General Washington said, "I hold the maxim no less applicable to public than to private affairs, that honesty is always the best policy."*

valor—bravery, courage (L *valere*, to be strong)

*The **valor** of Florence Nightingale and her corps of 38 dedicated nurses during the Crimean war is legendary.*

*Discretion is sometimes the better part of **valor**, such as when encountering a jaguar.*

venue—locale of a legal case, sporting event or drama (L *venir*, to come)

*Defense attorneys requested a change in **venue** because of the intensive publicity surrounding the sensational murders.*

*Atlanta was chosen to be the **venue** of the summer Olympic games in 1996.*

verbatim—word for word, following the original exactly (L *verbum*, word)

*Court and hearing stenotypists are **verbatim** reporters, some of whom use both stenotype machines and tape recorders.*

*When quotations are used, they should be either **verbatim** or paraphrased accurately.*

verbose—talkative, wordy, tedious (L *verbosus*, wordy)

*Garmond was as **verbose** in his books as he was laconic in speech.*

Thalia's **verbosity** *in class seemed to encourage the other students to speak up.*

verdant—green, leafy, fresh (MF *verdoyant*, to grow green, from L *viridis*, from *virere*, to be green)

If you want to see **verdant** *life, go to the botanical gardens in any large city.*

New Jersey is called the "Garden State" because of its **verdant** *fields of delicious vegetables.*

versatile—multitalented, flexible, many-sided (L *versari*, to turn, change)

Plastic is among the most **versatile** *of materials for every kind of industry.*

Because of his legendary **versatility** *and originality, as well as his tremendous body of work, Picasso is considered the foremost artist of the 20th century.*

vertigo—dizziness (L *vertere*, to turn)

The unforgettable motion picture **Vertigo***, starring Jimmy Stewart, depicts in frightening detail the plight of a man who is afflicted with* **vertigo** *and acrophobia but who risks his life to save another's.*

During a steep takeoff, a Navy pilot suffered **vertigo** *and unknowingly forced his jet into a dive.*

vicarious—substituting, delegated (L *vicarius*, from *vicis*, change)

Imagination is the most fertile originator of **vicarious** *joy or sorrow.*

*Parents take **vicarious** pleasure in the successes of their children.*

viral—relating to or caused by a virus (L *virus*, slimy liquid, poison)

*A wave of **viral** pneumonia swept through the entire hospital.*
*Researchers in genetics and cancer are investigating the composition of **viruses** that cause epidemics.*

virile—male, manly, powerful, forceful, decisive (L *vir*, man)

*He considered it **virile** to run every marathon race in every city on the East Coast.*
*Now in his 60s, Sean Connery is as **virile** as ever.*

The noun is **virility**.

vivacious—lively, sparkling (L *vivere*, to live)

***Vivacious** describes Bonnie's conversation and her outlook on life.*

The noun is **vivacity**.

vocation—calling, profession, inclination (L *vocatio*, summons, bidding)

*Franz Liszt took minor orders in the Roman Catholic Church and could have spent his life as an abbé, but he is better known for his **vocation** as a composer.*

vociferous—vehement, boisterous, raucous (L *vociferari*, to cry out)

> *Most musical comedies were too **vociferous** for Harriet's taste.*
> *The **vociferous** audience intimidated the inexperienced and high-strung cast.*

voluble—talkative, changeable, fluent, glib (L *volvere*, to turn, revolve, roll)

> ***Voluble** people are often hiding something.*
> *Leonhard was so **voluble** that he monopolized eight of every ten conversations.*

> The noun is **volubility**.

voracious—all-devouring, all-consuming (L *vorare*, to devour)

> *Joseph Conrad's facility with English stemmed from his **voracious** reading of books in both Polish and English.*
> *Most professional athletes have **voracious** appetites that would make a weight-watcher shudder.*

> The noun is **voracity**.

vortex—swirling center of activity (L *vertex, vortex*, whirl, whirlpool)

> *Election headquarters became the **vortex** of enthusiastic volunteers running hither and yon with posters and banners and pamphlets.*
> *A tornado is a violent, destructive whirlwind formed around a **vortex**.*

vulgate—common language, language of the people (L *vulgata*, common, ordinary, from *vulgare*, to make known, publish, from *vulgus*, mob, common people)

> *Eric Hoffer, a stevedore-turned-author, uses the* **vulgate** *in his books like no one else.*
> *An edition of the Latin Bible used by the Roman Catholic Church is known as the* **Vulgate***.*

vulpine—like a fox, crafty (L *vulpes*, fox)

> *In* The Pink Panther, *Inspector Clouseau (played by Peter Sellers) thinks he is stalking his prey in a* **vulpine** *way, but he succeeds only in being comic.*

W

waive—forsake, abandon, give up (ONF *weyver*, from *waif*, lost, unclaimed)

> *Johnson* **waived** *his right to extradition when it became clear that Florida would insist on trying him for his misdeeds.*

wanton—willful, unrestrained, reckless (ME *wan*, deficient, *towen*, from *teen*, to train, discipline)

> *Riots marked the* **wanton** *disregard of the treaty between the two nations.*
> **Wanton** *spending brought ruin to the family.*

wherewithal—means, money, resources (ME)

> *To be a power in Wall Street, one must have the* ***wherewithal***.
> *Alexander Fleming had the* ***wherewithal*** *to win a Nobel Prize in medicine.*

This word is not pronounced *wear-with-ALL*. The accent is on the second syllable: *wear-WITH-al*.

whitewash—cover up, gloss over

> *The high officials responsible for the Watergate scandal tried to* ***whitewash*** *the entire affair.*

wittingly—knowingly, deliberately (ME, from *witen*, to know)

> *Forgery is fraud done* ***wittingly***.
> *Laura, with her poor eyesight, had* ***unwittingly*** *snubbed her best friend at a party.*

wreak—to punish, drive out, inflict (ME *wreken*)

> *A diet high in cholesterol can* ***wreak*** *havoc with the health of susceptible people.*
> *Earthquakes, volcanic eruptions, and tidal waves have* ***wreaked*** *catastrophes and killed millions of people over the centuries.*

X

English words and proper names beginning with *x* are pronounced as if they begin with *z*.

xenophile—one who is attracted to strange or foreign people, customs, manners (Gk *xenos*, stranger, *philos*, loving, dear, beloved)

> *Xenophiles make the best world travelers.*

xenophobia—fear of strangers or foreigners, or of anything strange or foreign (Gk *xenos*, stranger, *phobia*, fear)

> *Xenophobia is a real handicap in a pluralistic society, because it limits the possibility of learning new things and becoming acquainted with new people.*

xerography—dry copying (Gk *xeros*, dry, *graphein*, to write, print)

> *Before xerography, secretaries made multiple carbon copies of each page; that was B.C. (before computers) and cumbersome.*

xylography—wood engraving or printing, woodcut (Gk *xylon*, wood, *graphein*, to write)

> *Her hobby, xylography, became a lucrative occupation when she branched out into making portraits on wood.*

Y

YAG—(*yttrium-aluminum*-garnet) a synthetic gemstone

> *YAG is used in laser surgical technology.*

The element yttrium is so named from Ytterby, Sweden, where it is found along with other rare-earth elements.

yeoman—characterized by great effort and usefulness (ME *yoman*)

> *The ambassadors did a* **yeoman** *job in completing the delicate negotiations between the two countries.*

Z

zeal—enthusiasm, passion, fervor (Gk *zelos*)

> *The chess club spared no effort in its* **zeal** *to win the national championship.*
>
> *The* **zeal** *of the Egyptologist Champollion led him and others to decipher the three-language inscription on the Rosetta stone.*

The adjective is **zealous**.

zenith—highest point, peak, summit (ML, from OSp *zenit*)

> *Sir Arthur Conan Doyle's reputation as an author reached its* **zenith** *with the Sherlock Holmes stories.*

Doyle was also an ophthalmologist, but he abandoned his medical practice to devote himself to writing.

zoology—study of animals (Gk *zoion*, animal, *logos*, study)

A current specialty in **zoology** *is genetics.*

Some fans of National Lampoon's Animal House, *the raucous 1978 comedy about college fraternity life starring John Belushi, went on to successful careers in* **zoology**.

This word, like others with the same root, is pronounced *zoh-OL-ogy*, not *zoo-ol-ogy*.

Word Roots

a, an (not, without)

achromatic	without color
ahistorical	not historical
amoral	without morals
anesthesia	without pain
anhydrous	without water
apathy	without feeling
aplastic	not easily molded
aseptic	sterile, without infection
atheist	godless
atoxic	not poisonous
atrophic	not developing, growing
atypical	not typical

ab (away from, apart, from)

abase	to lower, degrade
abdicate	to surrender, yield
abduct	to carry off
abhor	to loathe, reject
abnormal	not normal
abridge	to abbreviate, shorten
abrogate	to repeal, repudiate
absolve	to release, set free, vindicate, acquit

ac, ad, af, ag, al, ap, as, at (to, toward, adjacent to)

By the process of assimilation, *ad* becomes *ac*, *af*, etc., to conform to the first consonant in the next syllable.

accede	to agree
accelerate	to speed up
accept	to take, receive
acclaim	praise
acclimate	to adjust to climate
accumulate	to gather, collect
adapt	to adjust, accommodate
adept	expert, skilled
adequate	sufficient
adhere	to stick, maintain loyalty
adjacent	near, nearby
adjudicate	to judge, settle finally
admonish	to reprove, chide
affiliate	an associate, subsidiary
affirmation	assertion, declaration
affluent	wealthy, rich
afforestation	replanting, reforestation
agglutinate	to unite, adhere
aggregate	to gather, collect together
allocate	to distribute
allusion	an indirect reference
apportion	to divide in proportion
apposite	highly appropriate

ascribe	to attribute
aspect	phase, appearance
assured	confident
attach	to fasten
attend	to give attention to
attractive	pleasing, personable

alg (pain)

analgesic	painkiller
cephalalgia	headache
nostalgia	homesickness, yearning for times past
podalgia	pain in the foot

ambi (both, around)

ambiguous	unclear, obscure, having two or more meanings
ambilateral	bilateral, affecting both sides
ambivalent	having contradictory feelings

ana (collections of information)

Americana	materials about America
Shaviana	materials about George Bernard Shaw
Darwiniana	materials about Charles Darwin

andr (man, male)

androcentric   stressing male points of view

androgen   male hormone

ante (before, preceding, earlier)

antedate   to precede

antepartum   the period before childbirth

anterior   near the front

anti (against, opposed to, rival)

anticipate   to give early thought

anticlimax   a letdown, disappointing event

antidote   remedy for poisoning

anti-Jacobin   opponent of the Jacobins

antithesis   opposed or contrasting ideas

aqua (water)

aquacade   water extravaganza, spectacle

aquamarine   blue-green, blue-green gemstone

aqueous   watery

aquifer   water-bearing soil

be (on, around, over, thoroughly)

bedeck	to ornament
bedevil	to annoy, pester
befriend	to be kindly to, make a friend
befuddle	to bewilder
berate	to scold, reprimand vigorously

bi (two, twice)

bicameral	having two chambers
bifurcate	to separate into two parts
bilateral	having two sides
bipartisan	composed of two parties
bisect	to divide, cut in two

bio (life, living)

biochemistry	relating to chemical actions in life processes
biology	the science of life
biolith	rock of organic origin

capit (head)

capitation	poll tax
capitulate	to surrender, yield
recapitulate	to sum up

cent (hundred)

century	100 years
bicentennial	200th anniversary
centimeter	1/100th of a meter

circum (around, about)

circumnavigate	to go completely around
circumscribe	to draw a line around
circumvent	to frustrate

col, com, con, cop, cor (with, together, jointly)

By the process of assimilation, *com* becomes *col*, *con*, etc., to conform with the first consonant in the next syllable.

accommodate	to adjust, make fit
collate	to gather in an orderly way
collingual	using the same language
colleague	associate, coworker
commend	entrust, praise
commingle	to mingle or mix together
commiseration	sympathy
concur	to agree, unite
condominium	common ownership
correlate	to establish reciprocal relations
corroborate	to confirm

contra (against, opposed to)

contradict	dispute, disagree
contrary	opposite, opposed, perverse, ornery
contravene	deny, contradict, disregard, dispute

corp (body)

corps	special or elite group
corporal	bodily
corporeal	physical, material, opposed to spiritual
corpus delicti	the body of crime, evidence
habeas corpus	protection against unlawful imprisonment
incorporate	to unit with, combine

crypt (secret, hidden)

cryptic	mysterious, enigmatic
cryptofascist	one having secret fascist sympathies
cryptography	art of reading code messages

de (not, opposite of, reverse)

debase	to degrade, depreciate
deemphasize	to play down, reduce in importance

defuse	to remove the fuse
dehydrate	to remove water or moisture, dry
dejected	dispirited, discouraged
deprecate	to disapprove
desultory	random, intermittent, erratic

derm (skin)

epidermis	outermost layer of skin
dermatology	science dealing with skin and skin disorders
dermatoid	resembling skin
pachydermatous	thick-skinned

dis, dys (not, reverse, deprive of, opposite of)

disconsolate	downcast, dejected
discrete	distinct, separate, detached
disquiet	disturbance
dissuade	to urge or advise against
dysfunction	abnormal or impaired function

e, ex (out of, away, not, missing, absent)

edentate	toothless
elude	escape
ephemeral	fleeting, transient

eviscerate	disembowel
exacerbate	to aggravate, make worse, embitter
exorcise	to drive out
extirpate	to eradicate, exterminate

equi (equal)

equanimity	composure, poise
equidistant	equally distant
equilibrium	balance
equitable	fair, even
equivocation	uncertainty, lie, prevarication

erg (work)

erg	a unit of energy
ergomania	excessive devotion to work
ergophobia	abnormal fear or dislike of work
synergy	cooperation, working together

escent (becoming, beginning)

incandescent	becoming white or hot
nascent	being born
obsolescent	becoming outdated, obsolete
renascent	being reborn

extra (beyond, outside)

extracurricular	outside of regular duties, obligations
extraneous	unrelated, irrelevant
extravagant	excessive

fold (multiplied by, times)

manifold	many, numerous, varied
tenfold	multiplied by ten
twofold	multiplied by two

gyn (woman, feminine)

gynecocentric	centered on women, stressing feminine interests
gynecology	branch of medicine dealing with women
misogyny	hatred or abnormal dislike of women

hex (six)

hexagon	figure with six sides and six angles
hexameter	poetic line of six metrical feet
hexapod	six-footed, an insect
hexasyllabic	having six syllables

hom (same, alike, similar)

homeopathy
system of medical treatment with drugs that can produce, in healthy people, symptoms like those of the disease being treated.

homeostasis
bodily or mental stability

homogenize
to blend, to make consistent

homologous
corresponding

homonym
word sounding like another but different in meaning, homophone

hydr (water)

anhydrous
waterless, devoid of water

dehydrate
to dry completely, remove water or moisture

hydrant
fireplug, faucet

hydraulic
operated by water

hydrophobia
rabies, morbid fear of water

hydrotherapy
treatment by means of water

hyper (super, above, beyond, excessive)

hyperactive
excessively active

hypersensitive
extremely sensitive

hyperventilatation
abnormal respiration

hypo (under, beneath, down, below normal)

hypochondriac	one overly concerned with illness
hypofunction	decreased function
hyposensitize	to reduce sensitivity, especially to allergens
hypotension	abnormally low arterial blood pressure
hypothesize	to make an assumption

iatr (medicine, physician)

geriatrics	study of aging, medical care and treatment of older persons
hydriatics	treatment by means of water, hydrotherapy
iatrogenic	produced by a physician or medicine
pediatrics	study, care and treatment of children

inter (between, among)

inter alia	among other things
intercede	to intervene
intercurrent	intervening
interdict	to forbid
interlingual	existing between two or more languages

internecine	characterized by great slaughter, deadly
intertwine	to entangle, interlace

intra (within, inward, on the inside)

intradermal	between layers of the skin
intraocular	within the eye
intravenous	by way of the veins

leg (law, legal)

legacy	inheritance, heritage
legatee	an inheritor
legislate	to enact laws
legitimize	to legitimate, make legal

less (without, free from, beyond the range of)

ceaseless	without a pause
doubtless	without a doubt
hapless	unfortunate, unlucky
ruthless	pitiless, without compassion
tireless	untiring

log (speech, word, discourse, thought)

logistics	the art or science of being in the right place at the right time
logodaedaly	arbitrary or capricious coinage of words
logomania	extreme talkativeness, logorrhea

magn (great, large)

magnify	to make larger or greater, exalt
magnanimity	generosity, greatness of spirit
magniloquence	highfalutin language, ostentation

mal (bad, evil, inadequate)

maladroit	awkward, clumsy, klutzy
malediction	curse
malefactor	evil person, criminal
malevolent	evil, vicious
malfeasance	misconduct, misbehavior, wrongdoing
malpractice	misfeasance, professional wrongdoing, dereliction of duty

man (hand, by hand)

manual	by or with the hand
manufacture	to make, produce

manumit	to free from slavery, liberate
manuscript	a writing by hand or other means

mega (large, strong, great)

megabit	one million bits
megabuck	one million dollars
megalopolis	densely populated area comprising several cities or metropolitan areas
megastructure	immense building with many stories

micro (small, enlarging, one-millionth part of)

microbe	extremely small organism
microgram	one millionth of a gram
microphone	device for amplifying or transmitting sound
microtext	text in microform

milli (thousandth)

millennium	a thousand years, era of supreme happiness
milligram	one one-thousandth of a gram
millivolt	a thousandth of a volt

neo (new, recent)

neogenesis	regeneration
neon	an inert gas much used to advertise
neonatal	relating to the newborn

noct (night)

noctambulist	sleepwalker, one who walks at night
noctilucous	shining at night, phosphorescent
nocturne	musical night piece

nomen (name)

cognomen	nickname, surname
nom de guerre	fictitious name
nom de plume	writing pseudonym
nomenclature	collective name, designation
nominal	in name only
nominate	to designate

ose (full of, having the qualities of)

grandiose	full of grandeur
otiose	vain, idle, without effect

paleo (old, ancient, primitive)

paleobotany	science of fossil plants
paleology	study of antiquities
paleotechnic	relating to ancient art or early industrial development

pend (hang)

depend	to rely on, trust
pendant	a hanging object
pendente lite	while litigation is going on
suspend	to hang, delay

peri (around, about, round)

pericardium	membranous sac around the heart
perinatal	occurring around the time of childbirth
peristyle	colonnade surrounding a building
periurban	area surrounding a city

phil (loving)

Anglophile	one who is partial to English ways
bibliophile	lover of books
Francophile	admirer of France or French customs

philanderer	flirt, fickle lover
philhellene	admirer of Greece or Greek culture
verbophile	lover of words

post (after, following)

posterior	toward the back
posthumous	occurring after death
postmillennial	occurring after the millennium
postprandial	occurring after a meal
postwar	occurring after the war

pre (before, preceding)

prejudge	to judge beforehand
preliminary	introductory
prelude	introduction, musical introduction
premeditated	considered, thought of beforehand
pretest	preliminary test

psych (mind, soul, spirit)

psyche	personality, self, soul
psychogenic	originating in the mind or emotions
psychopharmacology	study of effects of drugs on the mind
psychosomatic	relating to interaction between mind and body

quin (five)

quinquennial   occurring every five years, period of five years

quintuple   five times as much

quintuplicate   five identical copies

retro (back, backward)

retrieve   to regain, repossess

retrocede   to cede back

retrogression   movement, development backward

rubi (red)

rubefacient   causing redness

rubella   German measles

sang (blood)

consangineous   being of the same blood, ancestry

sangulnary   bloody, gory, bloodthirsty, murderous

sanguine   confident, optimistic

semi (half)

semiautonomous   mainly self-governing within a larger entity

semidiurnal   occurring twice a day

semimonthly	twice a month
semiprecious	not as valuable as precious gems

sub (under, less than, below)

By the process of assimilation, *sub* sometimes changes to conform to the first consonant in the next syllable.

subacute	between acute and chronic
subcaption	secondary headline
subdivide	to further divide
subjugate	to conquer
sublime	splendid
submerged	hidden, cryptic
subornation	crime of persuading a person to commit perjury
subpoena	summons to appear in court
subservient	servile, subordinate
subtle	delicate, elusive
subvert	to overthrow, destroy, overturn
succinct	terse, brief, concise

super (above, over and above, more than)

insuperable	unsurpassable
superabundant	much more than sufficient, superfluous
superficial	external, shallow, casual
superlatives	exaggerated expression

supersede	take precedence, replace
superstandard	above standard

syn (together)

synarchy	joint rule, sovereignty
synchronous	happening at the same time
syndicate	group of persons or firms
synergic	working together
synopsis	brief outline
synthesis	combination of elements
synthetic	artificially produced, artificial

tachy (rapid, fast, accelerated)

tachycardia	rapid heart action
tachygraphy	rapid or cursive writing, stenography, shorthand
tachymeter	surveying instrument to determine distances quickly

tom (cut)

anatomy	structure of animals or plants
appendectomy	surgical removal of the appendix
microtome	instrument to cut into small sections

tomography	planar recording of internal body images, body section roentgenography
tonsillectomy	surgical removal of the tonsils

tox (poison)

toxic	poisonous
toxicology	science of poisons and their effects on organisms
toxiferous	conveying or producing poison
toxiphobia	abnormal fear of being poisoned

trans (across, beyond, to the other side, through)

transatlantic	across the Atlantic Ocean
transgress	to sin, trespass
transient	fleeting, temporary, short-lived
translucent	transparent, clear, lucid
transmogrify	to transform
transmute	to transform
transpontine	on the other side of a bridge
traverse	to oppose, go across

ultra (beyond, excessive, hyper, super)

ulterior	hidden, latent
ultimate	extreme, farthest, earliest, utmost, basic, fundamental, last

ultimatum	final, last word
ultramarine	beyond the sea, vivid blue
ultramontane	beyond the mountain
ultrasonic	beyond the range of human hearing

under (below)

underact	to act with restraint
undercurrent	running under the surface, hidden
underdog	a predicted loser
underpin	to support, substantiate
underscore	to emphasize, stress
understate	to describe with restraint
underwrite	to confirm, guarantee, support

vert (turn)

convertible	changeable
invert	to turn inside out or upside down
perverse	corrupt, wicked, cranky, contrary
reverse	to turn around, revoke
versatile	adaptable, many-talented
versed	practiced, skilled
versicolored	variegated, of many colors
versify	to write poetry, relate or describe in verse or poetry
versus	against

vertex	highest point, acme, peak
vertical	perpendicular
vertiginous	dizzy, giddy, suffering vertigo

xen (strange, foreign)

xenocentric	favoring a culture other than one's own
xenon	an inert gas
xenophile	one fond of foreign things
xenophobe	one abnormally fearful of foreign things and people

xero (dry, arid)

xerography	electrically charged, dry copying
xerophilic	adapted to making do with little moisture
xerostomia	abnormal dryness of the mouth
xeroprinting	dry printing
xerothermic	being hot and dry

zo (animal)

zoic	relating to animals or animal life
zoographic	describing animals
zoomorphic	in the form of an animal
zoophobia	abnormal fear of animals
zoophyte	plant resembling an animal

Match Game

Choose the word or phrase in the right-hand column that best matches the numbered word. The answers are on page 189.

1. ameliorate	a. without a care
2. circadian	b. place next to
3. draconian	c. nerve
4. egregious	d. outrageous
5. foible	e. accidental finding
6. germane	f. boisterous
7. hubris	g. severe
8. insouciant	h. improve
9. juxtapose	i. terse
10. laconic	j. daily
11. mnemonic	k. fear of strangers
12. peripatetic	l. weak point
13. serendipity	m. relevant
14. vociferous	n. reminder
15. xenophobia	o. wandering

Word Aerobics No. 2

Fits and Starts

Choose the word in the right-hand column that most nearly fits the numbered word. The answers are on page 189.

1. mellifluous
   a. handy
   b. talkative
   c. honeyed

2. perquisite
   a. privilege
   b. necessity
   c. requirement

3. querulous
   a. talkative
   b. complaining
   c. nasty

4. reticent
   a. hesitant
   b. silent
   c. demanding

5. munificent
   a. grand
   b. generous
   c. moneyed

6. arcane
   a. secret
   b. cloister
   c. busy

7. flagrant
   a. aromatic
   b. distinguished
   c. notorious

8. honorific
   a. dignified
   b. gentle
   c. title

9. intransigent
   a. stubborn
   b. wandering
   c. official

10. malleable
   a. formidable
   b. hospitable
   c. pliable

11. taciturn
   a. quiet
   b. changeable
   c. talkative

12. torturous
   a. painful
   b. wrongful
   c. winding

13. voracious
   a. truthful
   b. devouring
   c. devious

14. euphonious
   a. tuba
   b. false
   c. tuneful

15. gratuitous
   a. needless
   b. appreciative
   c. hostile

Word Aerobics No. 3

As You Like It

Choose the most suitable word or words to fill in the sentence. The answers are on page 189.

1. These nutritionists require the dieter to adhere to their strict _____ for at least six months.
   a. regime
   b. sports medicine expert
   c. regimen

2. History has bestowed the _____ Father of Medicine on the Greek physician-teacher Hippocrates.
   a. emulation
   b. honorific
   c. honorarium

3. The Rolls-Royce careered down the mountainous, _____ road at breakneck speed.
   a. scenic
   b. tortuous
   c. toll

4. Finishing the Boston Marathon will _____ the average runner.
   a. exhilarate
   b. energize
   c. enervate

5. The pound symbol on a phone is also called a(n) _____.
   a. octothorp
   b. ampersand
   c. chevron

6. When she gave the job to her brother-in-law, the staff regarded it as _____.
   a. negligence
   b. nepotism
   c. sodality

7. The oracle's response was so _____ that no one could understand it.
   a. deleterious
   b. dismal
   c. cryptic

8. Negotiators had a tough job remedying the _____.
   a. panacea
   b. schism
   c. acrophobia

9. Although Beau was not as _____ as his gregarious uncle, he made many friends.
   a. worthy
   b. sanguine
   c. voluble

10. Susan was usually open-minded, but this time she was determined to be _____.
    a. adamant
    b. mercurial
    c. penitent

11. The proofreader was always careful to find any _____ in page proofs of the article.

    a. solace
    b. solecism
    c. iniquity

12. Carrying so many subjects at the same time was too _____ for Tom.

    a. otiose
    b. onerous
    c. versatile

13. The photographers took a _____ route through the jungle to find the birds they had come so far to study.

    a. circadian
    b. blatant
    c. circuitous

14. Differences between them were too _____ to be considered serious.

    a. infinitesimal
    b. impervious
    c. noisome

15. Debates should be lively and adversarial but not _____.

    a. palpable
    b. acrimonious
    c. pragmatic

Word Aerobics No. 4

Roots and Stems

Using the **Word Roots** *list beginning on page 157, choose the proper root to fit the blank spaces and complete the word in each sentence. The answers are on page 189.*

1. Luxurious, high-speed trains take you from Maine to California on a _ _ _ _ _continental journey.

2. Many carpenters and other artisans are _ _ _ _dextrous.

3. Being _ _lingual is a great advantage for people who work in the foreign service.

4. The younger campers sat in a _ _ _ _circle to hear and tell ghost stories.

5. Being of a cheerful and optimistic disposition, Arabella was _ _ _ _uine about the future.

6. Utilizing trash to make energy is con_ _ _ _ing waste into something productive.

7. The _ _ _ _atelist quickly snapped up all the stamps that bore the upside-down design.

8. Syn_ _ _ _ between coach and team members worked successfully for the entire season.

9. Bar_ _ _ _ _ _ _ is the medical treatment of obesity.

10. A host of festivities marked the sesqui_ _ _ _ennial of the museum.

11. Since the photographs are black and white, they are called _ _chromatic.

12. Bats are _ _ _ _urnal flying mammals that navigate by echolocation, a form of sonar.

13. Some older airplanes are now being _ _ _ _ _fitted with two "black boxes" and other modifications.

14. Montreal, like some other cities in the northern part of the hemisphere, has a bustling _ _ _terranean life, with shops, restaurants, and other comforts during the long, cold winters.

15. Random acts of kindness are _ _ _mendable.

Answers to Word Aerobics No. 1

1. h	9. b
2. j	10. i
3. g	11. n
4. d	12. o
5. l	13. e
6. m	14. f
7. c	15. k
8. a	

Answers to Word Aerobics No. 2

1. c. honeyed	9. a. stubborn
2. a. privilege	10. c. pliable
3. b. complaining	11. a. quiet
4. b. silent	12. a. painful
5. b. generous	13. b. devouring
6. a. secret	14. c. tuneful
7. c. notorious	15. a. needless
8. c. title	

Answers to Word Aerobics No. 3

1. c. regimen	9. c. voluble
2. b. honorific	10. a. adamant
3. b. tortuous	11. b. solecism
4. c. enervate	12. b. onerous
5. a. octothorp	13. c. circuitous
6. b. nepotism	14. a. infinitesimal
7. c. cryptic	15. b. acrimonious
8. b. schism	

Answers to Word Aerobics No. 4

1. transcontinental	9. bariatrics
2. ambidextrous	10. sesquicentennial
3. bilingual	11. bichromatic
4. semicircle	12. nocturnal
5. sanguine	13. retrofitted
6. converting	14. subterranean
7. philatelist	15. commendable
8. synergy	